INTERPRETING ISAIAH

FOR

PREACHING AND TEACHING

Kerygma and Church

INTERPRETING ISAIAH FOR PREACHING AND TEACHING

CECIL P. STATON, JR.

EDITOR

SMYTH & HELWYS PUBLISHING, INC.
Greenville, South Carolina

INTERPRETING ISAIAH

FOR

PREACHING AND TEACHING

International Standard Book Number 0-9628455-1-5

Smyth & Helwys Publishing Company, Inc.
P. O. Box 72
Greenville, South Carolina 29602

Contents

Preface to the Series

Smyth and Helwys Publishing presents the *Kerygma and Church* series in the hope of filling a void in literature available to ministers and churches. In particular, the series seeks to bridge the gulf too often separating the study from the pew and the academic classroom from the context of church life. The series legitimates its existence by the conviction that biblical scholarship has significant and relevant contributions to make to the ongoing life of the community of faith.

Because of its stated aim to connect the serious study of the Bible with the life of the church, the series intends to feature the contributions of persons who themselves are sensitive to the relationship between scholarship and church life. Whether the approach be primarily exegetical or expository, a sensitivity to both endeavors should be evident.

Both academicians and ministers/church leaders will find an avenue here to articulate their understandings of the Kerygma. The series further aims to be inclusive of the diversity existing within the total body of believers. While the series is expressly by Baptists and for Baptists, an inclusive spirit will also at times lead us to consider other perpspectives.

As students of Baptist history would expect from any endeavor invoking the revered names of (John) Smyth and (Thomas) Helwys, freedom of inquiry and expression is paramount for this series. A respect for scripture as authoritative religious literature bearing the Kerygma of the Word of God directs scholarship to listen carefully to what is said in order to learn how to respond faithfully. Beyond this healthy concern to "hear and obey," however, no other parameters are permitted to dictate the direction of study or the application of its findings. Through exegesis and exposition of biblical texts, the works of this series will strive to connect the Kerygma of God with the Church of God.

The Editors
Greenville, SC

Preface

Abraham J. Heschel, the great Jewish scholar of the Hebrew Bible, described the prophets of ancient Israel as "some of the most disturbing people who have ever lived." The prophets have always been troubling and yet fascinating to this student of the Old Testament. When studied carefully, the words of the great prophets of Israel almost seem to leap off their pages, demanding to be heard again and again by every new generation of the people of God.

It is an honor to present this collection of sermons, articles, and commentaries which have as their focus one of the best known and most loved Old Testament writings, the book of Isaiah. Each contributor is a Baptist sharing faith in Christ, reverence for scripture, and a commitment to freedom of inquiry under the leadership of the Holy Spirit. This collection represents a delightful diversity of approach, style, and assessment of themes by exceptionally capable ministers and scholars who are dedicated to connecting the serious study of the Bible with the life of the church. Each writer believes that Isaiah deserves to be read and heard as a word of God for people of faith today.

I express my appreciation to these contributors for their enthusiastic response to this project. I am honored by their willingness to trust me to present the fruit of their study and preparation for Christian proclamation. I am grateful to Smyth & Helwys for the privilege of bringing these gifted ministers together and for the forum to present this material by Baptists for Baptists.

My special thanks go to Wendy Thrift and Catherine Staton, my wife, for their help in typing portions of the manuscript. I also express my gratitude to my colleague Dr. Scott Nash for his invaluable assistance and suggestions during the planning and editing of this book; and to Ronald D. Jackson, managing editor of Smyth & Helwys, I express my thanks for helpful suggestions and encouragements along the way.

I believe this publication will prove useful for those who turn to Isaiah with the task of preaching and teaching in mind. Furthermore, it is my desire that this book may stimulate listening, conversation, and encouragement among us, as the people of faith continue to listen for a word from God from the anthology of prophetic writings known as Isaiah.

Cecil P. Staton, Jr.
Ailey, Georgia
Epiphany 1991

Biographical Notes

Contributors include:

Charles B. Bugg is the Carl E. Bates Professor of Christian Preaching, The Southern Baptist Theological Seminary, Louisville, Kentucky. He is a graduate of Stetson University and The Southern Baptist Theological Seminary. Before his present position, Dr. Bugg was Pastor of First Baptist Church, Augusta, Georgia.

Tere Tyner Canzoneri is a Pastoral Counselor in Atlanta, Georgia. The Reverend Mrs. Canzoneri, daughter of missionary parents and daughter-in-law, niece, granddaughter and great-granddaughter of ministers, is a graduate of Mercer University, Candler School of Theology, and the University of Georgia.

William Henry Crouch is Pastor of Providence Baptist Church, Charlotte, North Carolina. He is a graduate of Mars Hill College, Wake Forest University, and The Southern Baptist Theological Seminary, and in 1981 received Wake Forest University's Doctor of Divinity degree. Prior to his present pastorate, Reverend Crouch served churches in Kentucky, Mississippi, and North Carolina.

Paul D. Duke is Senior Pastor of Kirkwood Baptist Church, Kirkwood, Missouri. He is a graduate of Samford University and The Southern Baptist Theological Seminary and previously held pastorates in Kentucky. Dr. Duke delivered the H. I. Hester Lectures on Preaching at Golden Gate Baptist Theological Seminary in 1988, and at Midwestern Baptist Theological Seminary in 1989.

Thomas H. Graves is President of the Baptist Theological Seminary at Richmond, Virginia. He is a graduate of Vanderbilt University, The Southern Baptist Theological Seminary, and

Yale Divinity School. Dr. Graves has previously served as a campus minister and has served churches in Kentucky, Florida, and North Carolina. Prior to his present position, he was Senior Minister at St. John's Baptist Church in Charlotte, North Carolina.

Stan Hastey is Executive Director of the Southern Baptist Alliance, Washington, D.C. Dr. Hastey is a graduate of Oklahoma Baptist University and The Southern Baptist Theological Seminary. Before his present position he served as Bureau Chief for Baptist Press in Washington, D.C. and as Director of Information Services and Director of Denominational Services for the Baptist Joint Committee on Public Affairs.

Peggy A. Haymes is Associate Minister of the College Park Baptist Church, Greensboro, North Carolina. Reverend Haymes is a graduate of Furman University and Southeastern Baptist Theological Seminary.

Roy L. Honeycutt is President of The Southern Baptist Theological Seminary, Louisville, Kentucky. He is a graduate of Mississippi College, The Southern Baptist Theological Seminary, and the University of Edinburgh. Prior to his present position, Dr. Honeycutt served as Provost, Dean, and Professor of Old Testament at The Southern Baptist Theological Seminary, and as Academic Dean at Midwestern Baptist Theological Seminary.

Marion D. Lark is Senior Minister of the First Baptist Church, Henderson, North Carolina. He is a graduate of Furman University and Southeastern Baptist Theological Seminary. Dr. Lark served churches in both North and South Carolina before his present position.

Bill J. Leonard is the William Walker Brooks Professor of American Christianity at The Southern Baptist Theological Seminary, Louisville, Kentucky. He is a graduate of Texas Wesleyan College, Southwestern Baptist Theological Seminary, and Boston University. He previously served as a pastor in Massachusetts.

W. Randall Lolley is Pastor of First Baptist Church, Greens-
boro, North Carolina. He is a graduate of Samford University,
Southeastern Baptist Theological Seminary, and Southwestern
Baptist Theological Seminary. Dr. Lolley was President of
Southeastern Baptist Theological Seminary from 1974 to 1988.
He previously served congregations in Texas and North
Carolina.

Molly T. Marshall-Green is Associate Professor of Theology at
The Southern Baptist Theological Seminary, Louisville, Ken-
tucky. The Reverend Dr. Marshall-Green is a graduate of
Oklahoma Baptist University and The Southern Baptist Theo-
logical Seminary, and has done additional study at Cambridge
University, Tantur Ecumenical Institute, Jerusalem, and
Princeton Theological Seminary. Prior to the her present po-
sition, she served churches in Maryland, Oklahoma, Texas,
Arkansas, and Kentucky, and was a campus minister.

Rex Mason is Senior Tutor at Regent's Park College and is a
University Lecturer in the University of Oxford. Dr. Mason is
a graduate of Oxford University and The University of London.
Previously he served churches in England and Wales and taught
at Spurgeon's College, London.

Scott Nash holds the Barney Averitt Chair of Christianity and
is Chairman of the Division of Religious and Philosophical
Studies at Brewton-Parker College, Mount Vernon, Georgia.
He is a graduate of Centre College and The Southern Baptist
Theological Seminary and served churches in Kentucky before
his present position.

Alan Neely is Professor of Ecumenics and Mission, Princeton
Theological Seminary. He is a graduate of Baylor University,
Southwestern Baptist Theological Seminary, and American
University. Previously Dr. Neely served congregations in Texas,
Virginia, and Colorado. From 1963 to 1976 Dr. and Mrs. Neely
were missionaries to Colombia. Before taking his present
position at Pinceton, he taught at Southeastern Baptist Theo-
logical Seminary from 1976 to 1988.

James M. Pitts is Chaplain to Furman University, Greenville, South Carolina. He is a graduate of Furman University, Southeastern Baptist Theological Seminary, and The Southern Baptist Theological Seminary. Prior to Dr. Pitt's present position he served congregations in Virginia, Alabama, and South Carolina.

Charles E. Poole is Pastor of First Baptist Church, Macon, Georgia. He is a graduate of Macon Junior College, Mercer University, and Southeastern Baptist Theological Seminary, and in 1990 received Mercer University's Doctor of Divinity degree. He served churches in North Carolina and Georgia before his present pastorate.

Ron Sisk is Pastor of Tiburon Baptist Church, Tiburon, California. He is a graduate of the University of Arkansas, New York University, and The Southern Baptist Theological Seminary. Prior to his present pastorate he served churches in Kentucky and California and was with the Christian Life Commission of the SBC.

Cecil P. Staton, Jr. is Assistant Professor of Christianity at Brewton-Parker College, Mount Vernon, Georgia. Dr. Staton is a graduate of Furman University, Southeastern Baptist Theological Seminary, and the University of Oxford, and has served congregations in Georgia, North and South Carolina, and England.

Jon M. Stubblefield is Pastor of First Baptist Church, Shreveport, Louisiana. He is a graduate of the University of Arkansas and The Southern Baptist Theological Seminary. Before coming to his present position, he served churches in Arkansas and Kentucky.

Allen Walworth is Pastor of First Baptist Church, Huntsville, Alabama. He is a graduate of Samford University and The Southern Baptist Theological Seminary. Previously he served churches in Alabama and Kentucky.

Chapter One
Introducing the Book of Isaiah

by Cecil P. Staton, Jr.
Assistant Professor of Christianity
Brewton-Parker College
Mount Vernon, Georgia

The Hebrew Bible, commonly called the Old Testament, is divided into three major sections: Torah, Prophets, and Writings. The second division of the Hebrew canon, the Prophets, is further divided between the Former and Latter Prophets. The Former Prophets include the books of Joshua through 2 Kings. These books present the history of the conquest of the land to the time of the exile from a "prophetic" perspective. Prophetic figures play a prominent role in these books and are frequently the spokespersons who interpret this history for the reader.

The anthology of prophetic oracles known as the book of Isaiah stands at the beginning of the collection of fifteen books known as the Latter Prophets. This diverse collection embodies over one-fourth of the entire Old Testament, while Isaiah alone represents over one-fourth of the Latter Prophets.

The Latter Prophets may be further divided between the three Major Prophets (Isaiah, Jeremiah, Ezekiel) and the twelve Minor Prophets, sometimes called the Book of the Twelve.[1] Whereas in antiquity the Major Prophets required separate scrolls because of their size, the Minor Prophets were often found together on one scroll. This entire collection, known in Hebrew as *Nabiᵓ im* ("Prophets"), was gradually brought together over several hundred years (fifth to second centuries B.

1

C.) and was embraced by Judaism as authoritative writings before the time of Christ. The New Testament refers to the Old Testament as "the law and the prophets" (see, for example, Matt 5:17).[2] This collection of prophetic books was an important part of the scriptures of early Christians before the New Testament was written, beginning about the middle of the first century A. D.

What is a Prophet?

Before turning to the book of Isaiah, it may helpful to begin with the question, "What is a prophet?" This is necessary because of our modern usage of the words "prophet" and "prophecy." For example, someone reading the predictions for the new year in a supermarket tabloid may find the prognosticator referred to as a "prophet" or "prophetic." Indeed, this is the most common modern definition of "prophet." A prophet is commonly thought to be someone who predicts the future. But is this popular definition of prophecy an accurate reflection of biblical texts which describe the role of prophecy in ancient Israelite society?

There are several words associated with prophetic activity in the Old Testament.[3] Perhaps the oldest of these is the Hebrew word usually translated "seer" (*ro'eh* from the verb *ra'ah* "to see"). The title "seer" is not used frequently in the Old Testament, although it is applied to Samuel, an important early prophet (1 Sam 9:11, 18, 19; see further 2 Chr 16:7-10 and Isa 30:10). 1 Samuel 9:9 explains, "Formerly in Israel, anyone who went to inquire of God would say, 'Come let us go the seer'; for the one who is now called a prophet was formerly called a seer." The word itself may suggest that the seer received oracles or divine messages during dreams or visions (1 Sam 3:2-18). The seer was consulted in order to ask questions of God or to gain information for which access to God was required (1 Sam 9:5-21).

The Hebrew word translated "visionary" (*hozeh* from another verb "to see" *hazah*) also suggests one who obtained revelations through visions. Amos is called a "visionary" by Amaziah in Amos 7:12. This term is used for those prophets who support the Jerusalem theological and political establishments in the oracles of Micah (3:7) and Isaiah (29:10, 30:10) which are critical of institutional prophets.

The most frequent Hebrew word translated "prophet" is *nabi²*, used over 300 times in the Old Testament. The word *nabi²* probably derives from the verb *nb²* which means "to bubble up, pour forth." The prophets were thus those who bubbled forth or poured forth their words or messages under the excitement of inspiration.

Although it is difficult to distinguish major differences between these words on the basis of their usage, apparently in time *nabi²* became the most common title for the prophet. At one time or another all three are used to refer to the same phenomenon, the presence of intermediaries between God and the people of ancient Israel.

The Role of Prophecy in Ancient Israel

The search for a definition of prophet or prophecy requires further consideration of the role of the prophet in ancient Israelite society.[4] An inquiry into the role of prophets, however, is more difficult than one might think. Prophecy in ancient Israel evolved over several centuries before reaching its heyday in the two hundred year period between 750 and 550 B.C., the time of many of the classical writing prophets.

In the pre-monarchical and early monarchical periods of Israel prophecy was largely ecstatic in nature. When Saul, for example, came upon David and Samuel at Ramah, he was possessed by the Spirit of God: "As he was going he fell into a prophetic frenzy,.... And he too stripped off his clothes, and he too fell into a frenzy before Samuel. He lay naked all that day and all that night. Therefore it is said, 'Is Saul also among the prophets?'" (1 Sam 19:23-24). This strange behavior is viewed as characteristic of prophetic activity. This interesting text harkens back to Samuel's announcement at the anointing of Saul that "the spirit of the Lord will possess you, and you will be in a prophetic frenzy along with them and be turned into a different person" (1 Sam 10:6).

Although ecstasy was a common feature of early Israelite prophecy, references to such bizarre behavior as are found in texts relating to Samuel and Saul in the Deuteronomistic History (Joshua to 2 Kings) are more rare in the collection of writing prophets.[5] There are, however, references in later prophetic writings which suggest that Jeremiah delivered oracles during a state of ecstacy (Jer 4:19, 23:9, 29:26-27). This is true of Ezekiel as well (Ezek 2:2, 3:14-15, 22, 24; 8:1, 3; 11:1, 5,24; 33:22; 37:1; 40:1-2). Thus some prophets may have delivered their messages while in a state of ecstacy, or perhaps produced their oracles following their ecstatic experiences (see further Num 11:26-30; 1 Kgs 18:46).

Early prophecy in ancient Israel also involved clans or groups of prophets centered around a charismatic leader. So, for example, 1 Samuel 10:10 refers to a "band of prophets," presumably associated with Samuel. 1 Samuel 19:20 refers to a "company of prophets in a frenzy, with Samuel standing as head over them." Elijah was leader of a group known as "the company of the prophets" (1 Kgs 20:35, 2 Kgs 2:3ff). Later Elisha assumed the leadership of this group (2 Kgs 4:1, 38; 5:22; 6:1; 9:1). Members of the prophetic guild sometimes lived and ate together (2 Kgs 4:38-41; 6:1), though at other times members seem to have lived independent of one another (2 Kgs 4:1).

Textual evidence also associates some prophets with the royal court, especially during the early monarchical period. Nathan and Gad are mentioned in association with David's reign. Nathan is called a "prophet" (2 Sam 7:2) while Gad is referred to as both a prophet (1 Sam 22:5; 2 Sam 24:11) and as "David's seer" or visionary (2 Sam 24:11). Both may have served as something like a court chaplain during David's reign. Both functioned as intermediaries between David and Yahweh and are presented as either inquiring of Yahweh on behalf of the king or bringing Yahweh's message to David (see 2 Sam 7:4ff; 12:1ff; 24:1ff). Sometimes this brought the prophet into potential conflict with the king, as in the case of Nathan's famous parable of the ewe lamb following David's adultery with Bathsheba (2 Sam 11-12).

Moreover, there are biblical texts which suggest that certain prophets delivered their message in the context of the cult. The prophetic guilds may have functioned alongside priests in the worship of ancient Israel. Samuel, for example, is associated with the cultic centers of Shiloh, Bethel, Gilgal, Mizpah, and Ramah (1 Sam 3; 7:15-17). He fulfills a dual prophetic/priestly role before King Saul (1 Sam 13:8-15). Although in some cases no scholarly consensus has arisen, at one time or another it has been suggested that Isaiah, Micah, Nahum, Habakkuk, Ezekiel, Zephaniah, and Joel should be viewed as cultic prophets, or as having their setting in Israelite society within the cult.

Perhaps the most significant development in ancient Israelite prophecy, however, is the tendency over time for an individual to come forward as a lone prophet of Yahweh, the God of Israel. The isolated prophet of Yahweh often stood in opposition to the religious and political establishments as well as their families and other prophets (for example, Jer 15:10-21; 20:7-18; 23:9-22). This phenomenon is most clearly seen in the remarkable collection of fifteen books which make up the prophetic corpus of the Old Testament. The oracles of a number of select Israelite prophets were collected, preserved and passed on by disciples, later edited by still others, and eventually adopted in the post-exilic period (after 538 B.C.) as authoritative writings for Judaism. Later still, Christians also embraced them as authoritative for the life and faith of the Church and confessed that in Jesus Christ prophetic hopes were ultimately fulfilled.

A Definition

Any attempt to define prophecy should take into account the length and breadth of the Old Testament witness to the prophetic phenomenon in ancient Israel. Abraham J. Heschel, the great Jewish scholar, speaks of prophecy as "an interpretation of a particular moment in history, a divine understanding of a human situation." He writes, "Prophecy, then, may be described as exegesis [interpretation] of existence from a divine perspective."[6] Putting it more simply, B. Elmo Scoggin, Professor Emeritus of Old Testament at Southeastern Baptist Theological Seminary, defines prophecy as "courageous contemporary preaching."[7] Although interest in what Yahweh will do in the future is obviously present in prophetic texts, Israel's prophets were first and foremost messengers of God's word for their contemporaries, not fortune-tellers or future-predictors. Rather, they were forth-tellers.

The prophets were *courageous* in that they were often at odds with their fellow citizens as well as with religious and political leaders. Jeremiah, for example, was beaten and imprisoned because of the daring words he proclaimed concerning Jerusalem's destruction (see Jer 7, 26, 37). The prophets were *contemporary* in that they were mediators of God's word and interpreters of current events through the eyes of faith. Amos, for example, saw the abuses of the poor and needy during the otherwise prosperous and outwardly religious decade of 760-750 B.C. He boldly declared the judgment of Yahweh for the Northern Kingdom of Israel if the non-applied religion of the people and King Jeroboam II did not give way to the justice and righteousness demanded by Yahweh (see Amos 2:6-8; 5:21-24). And the prophets of ancient Israel were certainly *preachers* in the best sense of that word, concerned to communicate the message of God which sometimes became an overwhelming burden to them. Amos confesses, "The Lord God has spoken; who can but prophecy?" (3:8).

The prophets confessed that Yahweh called them from their various backgrounds to be God's spokespersons (Isa 6; Jer 1:4-10; Amos 7:14-15). They were granted continuing access to the presence of Yahweh (1 Kgs 22:19-23; Ezek 1). True prophecy in the Old Testament was always "courageous contemporary preaching" in contrast with those who cried peace when there was money enough, or who served as yes men for the king, telling everyone what they wanted to hear (Micah 3:5-8; Jer 14:13-16). The prophets came from every background, rich, poor, learned and uneducated, male and female (2 Kgs 22:14ff). When the Spirit of God came upon them they heard the cry, "Whom shall I send, and who will go for us?" Their reply was, "Here am I; Send me!" (Isa 6:8). The prophets were *courageous contemporary preachers.* To reduce them to the role of future-predictors is to misunderstand them and to overlook the important role they played as God's spokespersons. It is to ignore their inspiration as called messengers of a contemporary word from God, a word which continues to speak, challenge, convict, judge, and give hope to people of faith who embrace these words as words from God for their lives.

The Book of Isaiah and
Old Testament Scholarship

Where does one begin in the attempt to interpret the book of Isaiah? Concerning this, the great Old Testament scholar George Adam Smith wrote in 1888,

> No Book of the Bible is less susceptible of treatment apart from the history out of which it sprang than the Book of Isaiah; and it may be added, that in the Old Testament at least there is none which when set in its original circumstance and methodically considered as a whole, appeals with greater power to the modern conscience. Patiently to learn how these great prophecies were suggested by, and first met, the actual occasions of human life, is vividly to hear them speaking home to life still.[8]

Certainly this is no less true for students of Isaiah today. When carefully studied in its historical context, Isaiah continues to offer the community of faith a contemporary word from God.

Biblical scholarship is by nature a conservative enterprise. Biblical scholarship begins with tremendous respect for the biblical text and a yearning to hear what the author of the text originally intended to say. The integrity of the text demands that we hear its voice in its original context first. Then and only then are we able to hear and to interpret the text with soundness for our lives and our communities of faith. To understand the book of Isaiah and the message of this anthology of prophetic oracles, we must know something of the background which called forth these words from God through his prophets. The prophets were not isolated from their time, their people, their contemporary situation and its need. Rather, they were intimately involved with current events and caught up in them, seeking to bring God's word to bear upon their moment in time.

Beginning in the eighteenth century many interpreters of the Isaiah corpus began to suggest that the book had two independent sections: chapters 1-39, the book of Isaiah proper from the second half of the eighth century B.C.; and chapters 40-66 from the time of the Babylonian exile (587-538 B.C.). By 1892 the view of the German Old Testament scholar B. Duhm had become established as scholars now made a further distinction between chapters 40-55 from the exilic age and chapters 56-66 from the post exilic period (after 538 B.C. and the Edict of Cyrus II when the Jews were allowed to return to Jerusalem). The three sections of the book of Isaiah were designated Proto-Isaiah, Deutero-Isaiah, and Trito Isaiah, or simply First, Second, and Third Isaiah.

Although this view has been established in Old Testament scholarship for nearly one hundred years, the idea of multiple authorship for the material in Isaiah continues to cause alarm for some students of the Bible when first encountered. This is understandable because of the unfortunate gulf which all too often separates biblical scholarship from the life of the Church. The tradition that the book of Isaiah contains the prophetic messages of a single prophet from the eight century B.C. prevails, though scholarship has long recognized a protracted process, perhaps over nearly three hundred years, through which the anthology of material in Isaiah has passed before reaching its final form. Why have biblical scholars reached these conclusions regarding Isaiah? Is there any evidence to support their view? What does this say about the book of Isaiah and the inspiration of scripture? Does this devalue the book in any way? Does not the New Testament credit material from various parts of the book to a single prophet?[9] These and a whole host of other questions come to mind when this idea is first encountered.

Perhaps the most significant question is why did scholars eventually come to the conclusion that Isaiah is an anthology of prophetic oracles from different hands put together over a protracted period of time? This idea did not come about as a result of some desire to take a perfectly unified book and purposefully tear it apart. This idea occurred as a result of the careful reading of Isaiah itself. The reasons are *internal*. The different sections of the book suggest themselves following a close reading of the text.

In Mark 12:28-34 Jesus reminded the scribe who asked "Which commandment is the first of all?" that we are to love God "with all your heart, and with all your soul, and with all your mind, and with all your strength." There is nothing to be feared here. Biblical scholarship may be viewed as a way of loving God with the mind. It begins with the longing to hear the text. Yet scholarship takes seriously the barriers between the reader and a clear understanding of what the text means, barriers of culture and distance in time. Thus biblical scholars seek answers to questions which arise when one carefully encounters the text. It is the work of carefully studying the biblical text and its background in order to gain the necessary information to answer as best one can the question "What does this mean?"

Jesus said, "and you will know the truth, and the truth will make you free" (John 8:32). Christians have nothing to fear in the search for truth. The multiple authorship of Isaiah does not in any way lessen the value of this portion of scripture which repays careful study with a contemporary word from God. Questions of authorship, dating, and setting do not affect inspiration in any way. The answers to such questions, however, may aid our interpretation of Isaiah and prevent us from making the texts of Isaiah say something they were never intended to say. This reflects a healthy reverence for scripture and a desire to study it with integrity. There is nothing to fear here.

Contemporary biblical scholarship suggests that a thoughtful reading of Isaiah reveals important difference between chapters 1-39, 40-55, and 56-66: differences of time, difference of location, differences of mood, and differences of language and themes.[10] And these are readily apparent in the text of Isaiah itself. Let us look at each section in turn with the aim of discovering the historical setting of each section, its audience, and the central message of the prophet for the time in question. By connecting these major sections with their setting in time and their setting in the life of the community we will be in a better position to interpret the book of Isaiah for our lives and our communities of faith.

Isaiah 1-39

By and large the material contained in Isaiah 1-39 is associated with First Isaiah, or Isaiah of Jerusalem.[11] The name Isaiah is pregnant with meaning and may be translated,

"Yahweh gives salvation." The name of the prophet was a constant reminder that God was busy at the work of being savior.

Isaiah was married to a woman referred to as "the prophetess" (8:3) and was a father of sons to whom he gave symbolic names (7:3, 14; 8:3). On the basis of his call reported in 6:1-3, the first year of Isaiah's ministry would have coincided with the last year of King Uzziah's reign (742 B.C.). As there are no indications that the prophet was active after the Assyrian threat against Judah in 701 B.C., the ministry of Isaiah of Jerusalem may be dated between 742 and 701 B.C.[12] This agrees with the time frame of the superscription of the work (1:1) which places Isaiah's ministry during the reign of four Judean kings: Uzziah (783-742), Jotham (742-735), Ahaz (735-715), and Hezekiah (715-687). This represents an unusually long period of approximately four decades for Isaiah's ministry. During part of this period the prophet Micah, Isaiah's younger contemporary, would also have been active in Judah (compare Isa 2:2-4 and Micah 4:1-4).

Isaiah's ministry began in the death year of Uzziah (742 B.C.). Uzziah ruled from 783-742 B.C., having come to the throne at the age of sixteen following the murder of his father by conspirators (2 Kgs 14:19-21). Although little attention is given to Uzziah in 2 Kings (see 14:21-22; 15:1-7 where he is called Azariah), additional information may be found in 2 Chronicles (26:1-23) which suggests that Uzziah took advantage of a political and military void during his reign in order to expand the borders of Judah and to achieve political and economic stability for his small country. Uzziah was a successful king from the point of view of military expansion and economic prosperity.

Uzziah's son, Jotham, became co-regent about 750 B.C. when his father contracted leprosy. After Uzziah's death in 742, the year of Isaiah's call, Jotham became the sole king of Judah. 2 Kings 15 and 2 Chronicles 27 suggest that Jotham continued his father's policies and enjoyed similar success. This was a time of economic prosperity and optimism for the small kingdoms of Israel and Judah.

Thus the early years of Isaiah's ministry were a time of

economic prosperity: "Their land is filled with silver and gold, and there is no end to their treasures; their land is filled with horses, and there is no end to their chariots" (2:7). The prophet also suggests that it was also a time of idolatry and unfaithfulness to Yahweh: "Their land is filled with idols; they bow down to the work of their hands, to what their own fingers have made" (2:8). Although this was a time of unparalleled religious activity, Isaiah describes their faith as nothing more than non-applied religion:

> Hear the word of the LORD, you rulers of Sodom! Listen to the teaching of our God, you people of Gomorrah! What to me is the multitude of your sacrifices? says the LORD; I have had enough of burnt offerings of rams and the fat of fed beasts; I do not delight in the blood of bulls, or of lambs, or of goats. When you come to appear before me, who asked this of your hand? Trample my courts no more; bringing offerings is futile; incense is an abomination to me. New moon and sabbath and the calling of convocation—I cannot endure solemn assembly with iniquity. Your new moons and your appointed feasts my soul hates; they have become a burden to me, I am weary of bearing them. When you stretch out your hands, I will hide my eyes from you; even though you make many prayers, I will not listen; your hands are full of blood. Wash yourselves; make yourselves clean; remove the evil of your doings from before my eyes; cease to do evil, learn to do good; seek justice, rescue the oppressed, defend the orphan, plead for the widow (1:10-17).

As a result the prophet calls Judah to pass judgment upon itself. The "Song of the Vineyard" of Isaiah 5 confronts Israel with the image of a worthless vine which repays the vinekeeper's love and care with stink berries. The audience is asked what the vinekeeper should do. The only possible answer is destruction. The vine is fit for nothing and will be trampled down. By analogy Israel and Judah should expect the same: "For the vineyard of the LORD of hosts is the house of Israel, and the men of Judah are his pleasant planting; he expected justice, but saw bloodshed; righteousness, but heard a cry!" (5:7).

Ahaz replaced his father at his death in 735 B.C. and ruled to 715. It was about this time that the fortunes of Judah were to change for the worse. The void in international politics which had allowed Israel and Judah to prosper was quickly filled by Assyria. To understand this one must recognize that Israel and Judah occupied a very strategic narrow land bridge between the Mediterranean Sea to the west and the Arabian Desert to the east, between Mesopotamia to the north and Egypt to the south. Across this bridge merchants, soldiers, and travelers moved between the great civilization centers of Mesopotamia and Africa. This meant that Israel and Judah were almost always influenced by external powers and circumstances. Only in the absence of a world power did they prosper as independent kingdoms.

Shortly before Isaiah began his ministry, Tiglath-pileser III (745-727) became the monarch of a weakened Assyria. Immediately this aggressive king sought to put things in order at home so that attention might be given to recapturing Assyrian dominance over her neighbors. Eventually new military campaigns were orchestrated which led to a strengthening of Assyrian influence in the affairs of Syria and Palestine.

The events of 734-732 B.C. are of particular importance for understanding Isaiah 1-39 (see 1 Kgs 16; Isa 7:3-25; 8:1ff). Israel's king Pekah had joined forces with Rezin of Damascus in a campaign to end Assyrian rule. Pekah and Rezin wanted Ahaz, king of Judah, to join them. When Ahaz resisted, Rezin and Pekah joined forces against Judah in the so-called Syro-Ephraimitic War. Ahaz sent a plea for help to Tiglath-pileser, who responded by marching against Damascus. In 732 Damascus fell, its cities were destroyed, its citizens were exiled, and Rezin was killed (2 Kgs 16:9). Before Tiglath-pileser and his armies could march against Samaria, the capital of Israel, Pekah was assassinated by Hoshea (2 Kgs 15:29-30). Hoshea was recognized by the Assyrian monarch, but a portion of Israelite territory was also annexed by Assyria. Israel was also forced to pay tribute to Tiglath-pileser. According to Isaiah 7, the prophet strongly encouraged Ahaz not to fear the threats of Rezin and Pekah. Ahaz was told to place his trust solely in Yahweh. A young pregnant woman, perhaps the prophet's own wife, became the sign of God's presence with his people and the possibility of divine deliverance: "For before the child knows how to refuse the evil and choose the good, the land before whose two kings you are in dread will be deserted" (7:16).[13] Of course Ahaz found it impossible to believe the prophet with Rezin, Pekah, and their armies already stationed around Jerusalem. Instead, Ahaz turned to Assyria for help and the cost of this foreign aid was high. Judah became a vassal state of the Assyrian Empire. Ahaz was also forced to pay a heavy tribute to Tiglath-pileser for his assistance. As a sign of his subservience, Ahaz erected an Assyrian altar in Jerusalem using bronze from the Temple altar. He also dismantled some of the bronze equipment of the temple in order to pay tribute.

Further revolt against Assyrian dominance in the following years led to the final destruction of Samaria, the capital of Israel, and the end of the Northern Kingdom in 722. With the annexation of Israel by Assyria, Judah was left on the frontlines. Assyrian influence upon Judah and the heavy tribute demanded by Assyrian kings led Judah to join a revolt in 713-711. Isaiah 18:1-5 and 19:1-15 relate to this period. Although Egyptian aid was sought against the advice of Isaiah, the revolt was quickly put down by the new Assyrian leader, Sargon II. Isaiah declared that Judah should place her trust in God, not in the powers of Egypt.

During Hezekiah's reign a further revolt was attempted in 705/704 B.C. which may have coincided with the death of the Assyrian monarch, Sargon II. Again Egyptian military aid was sought out. Hezekiah also initiated many religious reforms (2 Kgs 18-20). By 701, however, Sennacherib, the new Assyrian king, made his way to Judah bringing destruction to the country and the surrender of Hezekiah (1 Kgs 18:13-16). Isaiah 36-37 relate directly to these events. Isaiah had assured Hezekiah that Yahweh would save Jerusalem if the King would trust the deity. The text reports that Sennacherib returned to his country and his army was devastated, presumably by a plague. In the end Jerusalem surrendered to Assyrian dominance once again, but it was not destroyed.

To summarize, the prophetic ministry of Isaiah of Jerusalem takes place between 742 and 701 and the setting is Judah. The mood and language of much of Isaiah 1-39 centers upon the theme of judgment. Isaiah spoke a courageous word concerning the lack of justice and righteousness during times of prosperity. He challenged the leaders and the people who embraced idolatry or a form of non-applied religion, rather than the demands of Yahweh, to choose faithfulness, justice, and righteousness.

Much of Isaiah's prophetic ministry is associated with the Assyrian crises of 734-732, 713-711, and 705-701. Isaiah proclaimed that Assyria's intervention in Judah's affairs represented the judgment of Yahweh upon his unfaithful people. Isaiah encouraged Judah to see crisis as a new opportunity to return to Yahweh in faithfulness. Isaiah, however, did not see Yahweh's judgment as his final word. He envisaged a remnant beyond judgment who would be true to Yahweh (10:20-23; 11:11-16). He looked forward to a time when there would be a Davidic king in Jerusalem who would surpass the weakness of Ahaz and Hezekiah and their tragic lack of faith (9:1-7; 11:1-9).

It is impossible to separate the prophet from his setting. His was a word from God for his day and hour. Living through the difficult times of the late eighth century B.C., Isaiah's call and message were for a specific purpose. Understanding this background aids the interpreter in understanding this prophet of Yahweh, his response to the call of Yahweh to "go to this people," and his word from God for them.

Isaiah 40-55

Isaiah 40-55 may be attributed to a second great prophet in the Isaiah tradition who worked during the exilic period, probably in Babylon. This refers to the time from the destruction of Jerusalem in 587 until the edict of Cyrus II in 538 which allowed the Jews to return from captivity to Jerusalem. By 539 the Babylonian Empire had crumbled, suffering defeat at the hands of the Persian king Cyrus II who had successfully joined the nations of Persia and Media. Cyrus' foreign policy was far different from that of the Assyrians and Babylonians who preferred to disorient conquered peoples by sending them into exile in unfamiliar places. Cyrus allowed his subjects to return to their homeland and even paid for the restoration of destroyed cities and temples (see Ezra 1ff). Thus the edict concerning the exiled Jews was issued in 538 B.C.

The reasons for suggesting this period as the date and setting for Isaiah 40-55 are apparent in the text itself. Whereas the names of Isaiah of Jerusalem's contemporaries are found numerous times in chapters 1-39, the only proper name of a historical personality found in chapters 40-55 is that of Cyrus who is described in his role as the one who releases the Jews by his edict (see Isa 45:1). There are also references to Babylon (43:14; 47:1ff) and the chief Babylonian deity, Bel (46:1).

The reader of Isaiah is left to draw one of three conclusions. Either Isaiah lived a very long time, that is well over two hundred years; or Isaiah, unlike other writing prophets was a future-predictor, even giving the exact names of the country and the foreign king who would rule hundreds of years in the future. A third and more reasonable possibility comes to mind which is in keeping with what we know about prophecy and with the internal evidence of chapters 40-55. We are dealing here with the work of different prophets from different times which has been brought together over a protracted period of time.

Moreover, the mood of chapters 40-55 changes so dramatically that one can hardly fail to notice it. The language of Isaiah 40-55 is obviously different from the chapters which precede it. Whereas judgment is spoken of as a future act of God in chapters 1-39, judgment is now in the past and the immediate future will bring a great salvific event, a new exodus. Second Isaiah begins,

> Comfort, O comfort my people, says your God. Speak tenderly to Jerusalem, and cry to her that she has served her term, that her penalty is paid, that she has received from the Lord's hand double for all her sins. A voice cries out: "In the wilderness prepare the way of the Lord, make straight in the desert a highway for our God. Every valley shall be lifted up, and every mountain and hill be made low; the uneven ground shall become level, and the rough places a plain. Then the glory of the Lord shall be revealed, and all people shall see it together, for the mouth of the Lord has spoken" (40:1-5).

This may suggest that Second Isaiah wrote just before the events of 539-538 B.C. His setting was the community of Jewish exiles in Babylon. God's message then consisted of words of comfort, encouragement, and restoration. Judgment was a thing of the past, merely a prelude to a new act of divine grace through the Persian King Cyrus II, Yahweh's anointed (45:1ff). Second Isaiah declares that every obstacle between Babylon and Jerusalem will be removed as a highway is prepared for God's journey to his people and his people's journey home (40:3-5). The focus of Second Isaiah is very clear. The sins of the exiles have been forgiven and Yahweh is now ready to bring about their salvation.

Although the identity of Second Isaiah remains completely unknown to us, something of his call may be preserved in 40:6ff:

> A voice says, "Cry out!" And I said, "What shall I cry?" All people are grass, their constancy is like the flower of the field. The grass withers, the flower fades, when the breath of the LORD blows upon it; surely the people are grass. The grass withers, the flower fades; but the word of our God will stand for ever. (40:6-8)

Within Isaiah 40-55 one encounters the four so-called "Servant Songs" (42:1-4; 49:1-6; 50:4-9; and 52:13-53:12) which have had an enormous influence upon the church's understanding of the ministry of Jesus Christ.

These four songs or poems are not easy to interpret. When viewed in their original context these poems obviously suggest that the prophet is referring to contemporary events, not something several hundred years in the future. The songs describe someone who is to bring God's law to the nations and restore justice. The identity of the servant does not seem to be described consistently in each of the poems, thus leading some to suggest that the servant is the nation (41:8-9; 49:3), others an individual (42:1ff), and still others both. At times the servant seems almost passive with respect to suffering (42:3; 53:7), while he is also described as assertive and conquering (42:1ff). No wonder the Ethiopian eunuch asked Philip concerning Isaiah 53:7-8, "About whom, may I ask you, does the prophet say this, about himself or about someone else?" (Acts 8:34). Whatever the case, one must agree with Columbia Theological Seminary professor James Newsome who writes,

There can be little doubt that in these Servant Songs Jesus found much conceptual framework for his own ministry, so that he is led to make the astonishing proclamation that the Messiah must suffer and die in order to fulfill the will of God (Matt 16:21-23). On these grounds Christians have understood that whatever contemporary figure(s), if any, the author of the Servant Songs may have had in mind at the time of their writing, the Servant of these poems is none other than Jesus Christ.[14]

The process by which Isaiah 40-55 was joined to chapters 1-39 remains a mystery. It may be assumed that it occurred very early, long before the Christian era, given that the present arrangement of Isaiah is found among the Dead Sea scrolls from Qumran (dated from about 200 B.C. to early first century A.D.) and in the LXX or Septuagint (a Greek translation of the Old Testament made during the third through first centuries B.C.). Newsome suggests,

This writer who was steeped in the prophecies of Isaiah of Jerusalem (and who was thus kind of a distant disciple), relied upon many of the theological concepts of the earlier prophet and used many of the same words and phases. And his words were, perhaps from the very beginning, considered by devout Jews worthy to be placed alongside those of the great prophetic contemporary of Kings Ahaz and Hezekiah.[15]

To summarize, Isaiah 40-55 is from a later prophet who pronounced God's message of a home-going and a hopeful future shortly before the Edict of Cyrus in 538 B.C. (45:1) This exilic prophet declared that judgment was in the past. The immediate future held a great salvific event, a second exodus, whereby the people would return to their ancestral homeland. The mood is no longer judgment; now it is comfort (40:1ff). Furthermore, Second Isaiah contains four Servant Songs which collectively look for a suffering servant who will bring Yahweh's law to the nations and restore justice.

Isaiah 56-66

Isaiah 56-66 is attributed to a third prophetic figure who worked sometime after 538 B.C., or during the post-exilic period. The location for Third Isaiah is Jerusalem and the audience for these words is the Jews who returned from exile to a Jerusalem critically in need of restoration. Exile and freedom from bondage are no longer the key images and there are no references to Babylonian deities or locations as in chapters 40-55. Rather again one finds references to Jerusalem (62:1, 6; 64:10; 65:18; and 66:10). The mood also changes as the prophet we call Third Isaiah brings God's message for the post-exilic Jerusalem community and its difficult circumstances.

What little we know about the post-exilic community in Jerusalem comes from the prophetic writings of Third Isaiah, Haggai, Zechariah, and Malachi and from the books of Ezra and Nehemiah. These writings reveal that life in Jerusalem after the return from Babylon was very difficult. Conditions were very poor. We read about draught and famine (Hag 1:10-11) and the animosity of those who had remained in the land (Ezra 4:4-6). There was opposition to the rebuilding of the city wall and temple. The beautiful new city promised by Second Isaiah (49:14-18) had not come to pass. Jerusalem was in ruins and there was little will to change it. Third Isaiah describes a city whose sins testify against it (59:12). Jerusalem was filled once again with liars, cheaters, and thieves: "The LORD saw it, and it displeased him that there was no justice" (59:15b).

Third Isaiah was a prophet in the tradition of Isaiah of Jerusalem who came to proclaim God's message for this troublesome time. It may have been that the people were discouraged because of the difficulty of life in Jerusalem in contrast to the life they left behind in Babylon. Third Isaiah's responsibility was to call a people who had become disinterested in God and worship to renewed faithfulness.

The prophet speaks of the further possibility of judgment if relationship with Yahweh is neglected (59:18-19). Third Isaiah attempts to communicate God's plan for his people which will be realized if they will embrace Yahweh fully. Jerusalem is bidden to arise, shine, and reflect the glory of Yahweh (60:1-4). Jerusalem's wonderful future is portrayed in terms of wealth, more returning exiles, and reconstruction (60:4ff). Jerusalem, once destroyed by foreigners, will in the future even surpass its former beauty during Solomon's era (60:17-18). Zion will be vindicated. God will do as he promised

(62:6-9): "See, your salvation comes!" (62:11).

Third Isaiah encourages the inhabitants of Jerusalem to become involved in the proper rituals of worship and to keep the sabbath (56:1-8). Those who involve themselves in the pagan practices of their neighbors will face further judgment (65:1-7). Proper fasting and God's desire for justice are described (58:1-9). When wickedness is rejected, when the oppressed go free, when there is bread for the hungry and shelter for the homeless,

> Then your light shall break forth like the dawn, and your healing shall spring up quickly; your vindicator shall go before you, the glory of the LORD shall be your rear guard. Then you shall call, and the LORD will answer; you shall cry for help, and he will say, Here I am (58:8-9).

Interestingly, the inhabitants of Jerusalem are not the only ones to be called to wakefulness and faithfulness. Third Isaiah also contains an appeal that God should reveal himself as in days of old. To a seemingly disinterested God the prophet cries:

> O that you would tear open the heavens and come down, so that the mountains would quake at your presence—as when fire kindles brushwood and the fire causes water to boil—to make your name known to your adversaries, so that the nations might tremble at your presence! When you did awesome deeds that we did not expect, you came down, the mountains quaked at your presence. From ages past no one has heard, no ear has perceived, no eye has seen any God besides you, who works for those who wait for him" (64:1-4).

Little can be known of Third Isaiah, though Isaiah 61:1-4 and 62:1 may preserve something of a call report. On the basis of interest in worship, fasting, and sacrifice it has been suggested that Third Isaiah may have been a priest. We must be satisfied, however, to remain in the shadows concerning this great prophetic figure. Much remains uncertain. Again we have few clues to the process by which Third Isaiah became attached to chapters 1-39 and 40-55. It may be assumed that it occurred at an early time.

To summarize, Third Isaiah was a spokesperson for

Yahweh during the difficult post-exilic period when Israel struggled to rebuild and define its future. This prophet encouraged renewed faithfulness to God during a time when faith was lethargic. Judgment would follow if proper worship was neglected. Appropriate interest in relationship with Yahweh and a faith embraced through living would bring God's blessing and healing for the community. Israel is called again to embrace its vocation in the world, to reflect the glory of Yahweh.

The Unity of Isaiah 1-66

Even this brief survey will suffice to show how different contexts lie behind the different sections of the book of Isaiah. There are obvious differences of time, setting, mood, language, and themes between chapters 1-39, 40-55, and 55-66. Identifying these biblical scholarship assists us in the task of interpreting these texts with more precision and soundness than was previously possible. We now know, as one scholar puts it, that "the author was speaking of actual, contemporary circumstances rather than speaking of some future events which, even to the prophet, was understood only vaguely."[16]

As stated above, the process by which this material came together to form the present book of Isaiah remains a puzzling question. Some have suggested that the material was brought together in time because First, Second, and Third Isaiah shared a unifying theological theme: Yahweh the Holy One of Israel (see, for example, 6:1-8; 41:1-4; 43:1-5; 57:15; 60:9).[17]

As helpful as this is, some scholars have recently come forward to suggest that the process by which the sixty-six chapters of Isaiah came together is far more complicated than previously recognized. For example, there are chapters in Isaiah 1-39 which seem to presuppose a knowledge of Second Isaiah and similarly there are passages in chapters 40-55 which allude to earlier chapters.[18] This may suggest a major reworking of the Isaiah corpus at a later time and not a simple joining together of previously independent parts.

Moreover, some would also remind us not to forget that Judaism embraced all sixty-six chapters of Isaiah as a theological unity and that this was the form in which Isaiah was accepted into the canon of Scripture.[19] The book contains only one superscription for the entire collection and this refers to the book as "a vision of Isaiah which he saw concerning Judah and Jerusalem" (Isa 1:1).[20] Certainly the literary boundaries between First, Second, and Third Isaiah are not clearly marked in the book itself. In fact, Second and Third Isaiah essentially have been divorced from their original historical setting in the canonical form of Isaiah. What is the interpreter to make of this? With respect to Isaiah 40-55 the Old Testament scholar Brevard Childs explains,

> First, by placing the message of Second Isaiah within the context of the eighth-century prophet his message of promise became a prophetic word not tied to a specific historical referent, but directed to the future. A message which originally functioned in a specific exilic context in the middle of the sixth century has been detached from this historical situation to become fully eschatological. In its new context its message no longer can be understood as a specific commentary on the needs of exiled Israel, but its message relates to the redemptive plan of God for all of history.[21]

In other words, the canonical shape of Isaiah reflects the use of this prophetic material as a contemporary word from God by Judaism in new contexts long after the historical referents for the material have passed. This is true of other portions of the Old Testament as well. The Psalms, for example, may originally have had very specific settings in the life of individuals or the community of faith. In the collection of the psalter, however, they have been torn away from their original settings so that they may be used by the community of faith in new contexts as expressions of praise and lament.[22]

Thus in the book of Isaiah we find that Second Isaiah's proclamation of the forgiveness of God (40:1ff) is set against Isaiah of Jerusalem's proclamation of God's judgment of his people. (1:5ff; 3:1ff). Judgment is shown to be but a prelude to a new act of grace on God's apart. The motif of a desolate country and a besieged Jerusalem (1:7-8) is contrasted with Third Isaiah's portrait of a Jerusalem vindicated and restored (62:1ff; 65:17ff). Isaiah unfolds around the scheme of "before and after" and "prophecy and fulfillment."[23] As a unified work, Isaiah shows us the purposes of God and their working out over three hundred years and says to us this is how God is. Isaiah invites its readers to consider the ways of God, the promises of God, and the possibilities for the people of God in every age. Through the images of judgment, exile, and home-coming the people of God are shown a portrait of the action of God in history in the lives of his people.[24] Through this the mind and purposes of God are revealed to ever new generations of the people of faith. Isaiah becomes a contemporary word from God for every new age, for those who stand in openness to God's future. Judgment, exile, and restoration continue to speak to later generations of the ways of the God of Israel who enters into relationship with his people and who takes that relationship very seriously.

On the following pages you will find a collection of ser-mons, articles, and commentaries by a number of competent and gifted Baptist ministers. These represent the outcome of their encounter with the text of Isaiah. Each writer shares the conviction that the anthology of prophetic utterances known as Isaiah offer to modern Christians a contemporary word from God for our lives. Listen and be challenged, and encouraged, and enjoy as we consider how the images found in the texts of Isaiah may become a contemporary word from God for us!

An Outline of the Book of Isaiah

I. Isaiah of Jerusalem: The Approaching Judgment
   A. Oracles of Judgment Concerning Judah and Israel 1:1-12-6
      1. Superscription (1:1)
      2. Rebellious Judah (1:2-31)
      3. Comparison of Before and After (2:1-4:6)
      4. The Song of the Vineyard and Six Reproaches (5:1-30)
      5. The Call of Isaiah of Jerusalem (6:1-13)
      6. The Immanuel Sign (7:1-25)
      7. The Mahershalalhashbaz Sign (8:1-22)
      8. The Prince of Peace: The Hope of a New King (9:1-7)
      9. Ephraim's Judgment (9:8-10:4)
      10. Assyria's Judgment (10:5-19)
      11. The Promise of the Remnant (10:20-34)
      12. The Shoot of Jesse (11:1-16)
      13. Songs of Deliverance and Thanksgiving (12:1-6)
   B. Oracles Against the Nations (13:1-23:18)
      1. Concerning the fall of Babylon and the Return from Exile (13:1-14:23)
      2. Concerning Assyria and Moab (14:24-16:14)
      3. Concerning Damascus and Ephraim (17:1-14)
      4. Concerning Egypt (18:1-20:6)
      5. Concerning Babylon, Edom, Arabia (21:1-17)
      6. Concerning the Destruction of Jerusalem (22:1-14)
      7. Concerning Shebna, Tyre, and Sidon (22:15-23:18)
   C. The Isaiah Apocalypse: God's Ultimate Plan (24:1-27:13)
      1. Universal Judgment (24:1-23)
      2. Yahweh's Victory: A Psalm of Thanksgiving (25:1-12)
      3. Songs of Yahweh's Victory and Deliverance (26:1-12)
      4. The Ultimate Deliverance of Israel (27:1-13)
   D. Concerning Judah, Israel, and their Neighbors (28:1-35:10)
      1. Against religious and political leaders (28:1-29)
      2. Against Spiritual Blindness (29:1-23)
      3. Against Alliance with Egypt (30:1-9)
      4. Hope for the Afflicted (30:10-33)
      5. Against Egypt (31:1-9)
      6. The Coming Righteous King (32:1-20)
      7. Liturgy of Praise of God (33:1-24)
      8. Judgment upon Edom (34:1-17)
      9. The Restoration of Zion (35:1-10)

E. Historical Appendix (36:1-39:38)
 1. Sennacherib's Invasion (36:1-37:38)
 2. Hezekiah's Sickness and Recovery (38:1-22)
 3. Visit of the Babylonian Envoys (39:1-8)

II. Second Isaiah: God's Forgiveness and Comfort, The Promise of a Homecoming (40:1-55:13)
 A. Comfort my People (40:1-11)
 B. God, Creator of the Universe (40:12-41:29)
 C. First Servant Song (42:1-4)
 D. The Victory of the Creator God who Redeems Israel (43:5-44:8)
 E. Idolatry Satirized (44:9-20)
 F. Israel is Forgiven (44:21-23)
 G. The Commission of Cyrus (44:24-45:13)
 H. Israel is Blessed; the Nations are Judged (45:14-47:15)
 I. Former Things; New Things (48:1-22)
 K. Return and Restoration (49:7-26)
 L. Third Servant Song (50:1-11)
 M. Deliverance is Near (51:1-16)
 N. God's Wrath is Past (51:17-52:12)
 O. Fourth Servant Song (52:13-53:12)
 P. Song of Assurance (54:1-17)
 Q. Song of Joy at the Anticipation of Restoration (55:1-13)

III. Third Isaiah: The Potential of a New Community of Faith (56:1-66:24)
 A. God's Desires for his People: A New Call to Repentance (56:1-59:21)
 B. The Mission of Zion: Shine! (60:1-62:12)
 C. God's Vengeance (63:1-6)
 D. Prayers of Intercession and Restoration and God's Answer (63:7-65:16)
 E. New Heavens and a New Earth (65:17-66:24)

Notes

[1] In the Hebrew Bible the book of Daniel does not belong to the division known as the "Prophets", but rather is found in the third division called the "Writings." In time the order of books was changed slightly so that in our English translations Daniel stands following the three major prophets and before the twelve minor prophets.

[2] The Canon of the Old Testament was completed by the addition of the Writings (Psalms, Wisdom, Literature, other worship literature, Chronicles, Daniel) around the end of the first century A. D., though certain of these books were certainly considered authoritative before this time. On the formation of the Old Testament see, E. Glenn Hinson, "Canon," *Mercer Dictionary of the Bible* (Macon: Mercer University Press, 1990): pp. 130-135.

[3] For a fuller discussion of these and other terms see Rolf Rendtorff, "nabi in the Old Testament," *Theological Dictionary of the New Testament* 5 (1968): pp. 796–812.

[4] See the important work of Robert R. Wilson, *Prophecy and Society in Ancient Israel* (Philadelphia: Fortress Press, 1980).

[5] Biblical scholars refer to Joshua to 2 Kings as the "Deuteronomistic History" because this record of the time from the conquest of the land (ca 1250-1200) until after the exile of Judah in 587 B.C. appears to have been written from the perspective of the theology of the book of Deuteronomy. Compare, for example, Deuteronomy 12 and 27–28 with the historians' explanations for the schism between north and south in 922 (1 Kgs 11), the fall of Israel in 722/1 B.C. (2 Kgs 17), and the fall of Jerusalem in 587 (2 Kgs 2 1ff).

[6] Abraham J. Heschel, *The Prophets* (New York: Harper & Row, Publishers, 1962), p.xviii.

[7] B. Elmo Scoggin, "Micah" in *Broadman Bible Commentary*, vol. 7. Edited by Clifton J. Allen (Nashville: Broadman Press, 1972), p.183.

[8] George Adam Smith, *The Book of Isaiah*, two volumes, revised edition (New York: Harper & Row Publishers, 1927?) I:xi–xii.

[9] Compare Matt 3:3; Luke 3:4-6 and John 1:23 with Isa 40:3-5; Matt 4:14-16 with Isa 9:1-2; Luke 3:4 and Matt 8:17 with Isa 53:4; Matt 12:17-21 with Isa 42:1-4; and Matt 13:14-15 with Isa 6:9-10.

[10] See James D. Newsome, Jr., *The Hebrew Prophets* (Atlanta: John Knox Press, 1984), p. 140.

[11] Today scholars regard certain sections of Isaiah 1-39 as deriving from later hands. It is beyond the scope of this brief introduction to deal with all such matters. For a brief survey of recent views see Rolf Rendtorff, *The Old Testament: An Introduction*. Translated by John Bowden (Philadelphia: Fortress Press, 1986), pp. 190ff.

[12] For a more detailed discussion of this period than can be presented here see John H. Hayes and Stuard A. Irvine, *Isaiah the Eight-Century Prophet: His Times and His Preaching* (Nashville: Abingdon Press, 1987).

[13] Isa 7:14 is often taken completely out of its context and viewed as a prediction of the birth of Christ. See Elizabeth Achtemeier's helpful treatment of this text in relationship to Luke 2:1-20 in *Preaching from the Old Testament* (Louisville: Westminster/John Knox Press, 1989), p.134.

[14] Newsome, p. 145.

[15] Ibid., p.139.

[16] Ibid., p. 177.

[17] Ibid., p.177.

[18] Compare 42:18f. and 44:18 with 6:9f.; 19:18; and 35:5. A more developed discussion of this issue may be found in R.E. Clements, *Isaiah 1-39*, The New Century Bible Commentary (Grand Rapids: Eerdmans, 1980), pp. 21ff.

[19] Among these voices is that of Brevard S. Childs. See his *Introduction to the Old Testament as Scripture* (Philadelphia: Fortress Press, 1979), pp. 316–338.

[20] See the helpful comments of Christopher R. Seitz in *Reading and Preaching the Book of Isaiah* (Philadelphia: Fortress Press, 1988), pp. 105ff.

[21] Childs, p. 326.

[22] See how this is true with respect to a particular psalm in my article, "'How Long, O Yahweh?' The Complaint Prayer of Psalm 13," *Faith and Mission* VII/2 (1990): 59-67.

[23] Childs, p. 330.

[24] See the interesting application of the images of exile and homecoming for contemporary American culture and religion in Walter Brueggemann, *Hopeful Imagination: Prophetic Voices in Exile* (Philadelphia: Fortress, 1986), pp. 1–7, 90–130.

For Further Study

Commentaries:

Clements, R.E., *Isaiah 1-39*, The New Century Bible Commentary. Grand Rapids: Eerdmans Publishing, 1980.

Kaiser, Otto, *Isaiah 1-12*. Translated by R.A. Wilson. Old Testament Library. Philadelphia: Westminster Press, 1972.

_____, *Isaiah 13-39*. Translated by R.A. Wilson. Old Testament Library. Philadelphia: Westminster Press, 1974.

Kelly, Page H., "Isaiah," *Broadman Bible Commentary*, vol. 5. Clifton J. Allen, Ed. Nashville, Broadman Press, 1971.

Muilenburg, James, "The Book of Isaiah" (40-66), *Interpreter' Bible*. vol. 5. Nashville: Abingdon Press, 1956.

Scott, R.B.Y., "The Book of Isaiah" (1-39), *Interpreter's Bible*, vol. 5. Nashville: Abingdon Press, 1956.

Watts, John D.W., *Isaiah 1-33*, Word Biblical Commentary. Waco: Word Books, 1985.

_____, *Isaiah 34-66*, Word Biblical Commentary. Waco: Word Books, 1987.

Whybray, R.N., *Isaiah 40-66*, The New Century Bible Commentary. Grand Rapids: Eerdmans Publishing, 1975.

Westermann, Claus, *Isaiah 40-66*. Translated by David M. G. Stalker. Old Testament Library. Philadelphia: Westminster Press, 1969.

Other Studies:

Achtemeier, Elizabeth, *Preaching from the Old Testament*. Louisville: Westminster/John Knox Press, 1989.

Blenkinsopp, Joseph, *A History of Prophecy in Israel*. Philadelphia: Westminster Press, 1983.

Brueggemann, *Hopeful Imagination: Prophetic Voices in Exile*. Philadelphia: Fortress Press, 1986.

Childs, Brevard S., *Introduction to the Old Testament as Scripture.* Philadelphia: Fortress Press, 1979.

Hayes, John H., and Stuart, A. Irvine, *Isaiah the Eighth Century Prophet: His Life and His Times.* Nashville: Abingdon, 1987.

Heschel, Abraham J., *The Prophets.* New York: Harper & Row Publishers, 1962.

Newsome, James D. Jr., *The Hebrew Prophets.* Atlanta: John Knox Press, 1984.

von Rad, Gerhard, *The Message of the Prophets.* Translated by D. M. G. Stalker. New York: Harper & Row Publishers, 1967.

Seitz, Christopher R., Editor, *Reading and Preaching the Book of Isaiah.* Philadelphia: Fortress Press, 1988.

Wilson, Robert R., *Prophecy and Society in Ancient Israel.* Philadelphia: Fortress Press, 1980.

Chapter Two
A Father's Heart
Isaiah 1:1-20

by William Henry Crouch
Pastor, Providence Baptist Church
Charlotte, North Carolina

Each individual views conditions and situations differently. Isaiah, a prophet of the eighth century B.C., saw the people of his day through the eyes of God. He was called to the task of waking them up to the spiritual meaning of the historical events that surrounded their lives. Israel was caught in the intrigues, conflicts, and struggles of their neighbors. They were blinded and indifferent to the real significance of their circumstances. The prophet saw God's strategy behind it all and knew it was neither accidental nor fate.

God was like a father who loved, cared for, and in the past had delivered his children. They had been called to be his servants in worship, to witness to the other nations, and to be on mission. So caught up with their own agendas, they had lost their vision as covenant people—a people blessed, conditioned on their keeping God's commandments.

A Father's Dilemma—Wayward Children

God called heaven and earth to witness the stubbornness of children "reared" and "brought up" in a privileged environment. In their rebellion and stubbornness they had forsaken their father and turned their backs on him. This chapter becomes an epitome of the whole message of Isaiah, as he pictures God as a father, overflowing with anguish, as he seeks to claim the allegiance of prodigal children.

It was Jesus who pictured God as a loving father and taught us to pray "Our Father." It was Isaiah in the Old Testament who urged this concept in his prophesy. His vision is a word from God who sees his covenant people as his children. Such a relationship makes him very personal, loving, caring. He has expectations for his children. He is concerned with Israel, Judah, and Jerusalem and has a dispute with them because of their lifestyle. Later, he would express this dilemma like this: "For my thoughts are not your thoughts, nor are your ways my ways, says the LORD" (55:8).

I had the privilege of having a Christian father. Living in his home was a tremendous heritage and a great privilege. He taught by words and example. Through the years to maturity, I experienced concern, grief, and frustration, as through exhortation he sought to guide me to certain conclusions about life. When I failed, pain, hurt, and disappointment were experienced. Punishment usually led to a feeling of displeasure or a loss of fellowship. He had such high expectations for each of his three sons that we were conscious of his watchful eye. Our burning desire was to please him and not to disappoint him by our lifestyle or our mission in life.

So, I read this passage in the light of a grieving father who pleads his case, his concerns, and his disappointments over his children. He is frustrated and angry. Yet he pleads with them to change their hearts and thus change their lives. He is not a ruthless deity, not a vengeful or remote God, but a loving and caring father whose heart is broken.

The Father's Sorrow: Isaiah 1:2-9

I can still remember times when my father looked at me in disappointment and disbelief that a son of his could have been so careless and thoughtless in certain situations.

As Isaiah begins, one can feel God's yearning heart; it is a sorrowful cry and the pathetic part is they do not even know what they are doing, nor do they understand even their rebellion. They appear to be living in a dull stupor. Children have been lost, gone astray, or perhaps even worse. Here is the agony of a father whose children ignore their parental upbringing. God's children have turned their backs on their father, not even recognizing him.

What has caused this alienation? They have a false sense of security and fail to see themselves as sinners. They have deceived themselves and therefore fail to see what was really happening to their nation and their relationship to God. The father takes issue with their assumptions and reminds them that only by his grace have they survived.

Their pride and self-deception led the way to rebellion. Their minds were dulled by materialism and sensuality and they became "a people laden with iniquity" (1:4). In this stupor, they could not discern the presence or activity of God. As they excluded God from their world and way of living, they became unsound from the "sole of the foot even to the head" (1:6). Very little regard was given to divine guidance or any effort to please God.

They were definitely ungrateful. Adopted as God's children and given favor by his grace and love, they failed to show appreciation. He had delivered them and brought them to maturity. They had turned their backs and in shame forsaken their heritage. For children to respond by ignoring this primary relationship is inexcusable.

They rebelled and forfeited their responsibility. This is seen as a deliberate, willful act. It denies the most elementary recognition of the one who has fathered them. They have forsaken the Lord and turned their backs on him.

"Your country lies desolate, your cities are burned with fire; in your very presence aliens devour your land . . . and daughter Zion is left like a booth in a vineyard" (1:7-8). Here is a clear reference to the historical situation, the Assyrian invasion, and the deliberate slaughter and destruction that followed. Isaiah saw it from a father's heart and interpreted it: "Ah, sinful nation." God's heart is full of indignation and hurt. His children are outwardly defeated and inwardly corrupt and they feel no sense of guilt. They have brought tragedy upon themselves; yet, they do not understand.

Only the mercy of a loving father has prevented utter destruction. I have stood with many a father at a jail, or in a courtroom, or at a hospital bed and felt with them the agony and pain they suffered because of the thoughtless behavior of a child in rebellion.

The Father's Rejection: Isaiah 1:10-15

Isaiah issues the warning that shallow worship can become a hollow mockery. Such hypocrisy is unacceptable to God who has the ability to see beyond the act to the very heart of the worshiper. Our attempts to gain God's favor by going through rituals of worship are vain and without success.

Our sin and rebellion put distance between ourselves and God. This relationship cannot be artificially restored. To go through habitual rituals void of meaning merits the rejection of God. He threatens to hide his eyes from them and close his ears to their petitions.

Amos, Micah, Hosea, and Jeremiah each in turn denounced forms of worship which have no influence on a person's handling of life. God is far more interested in right relations between his children than with the scrupulous regard for public worship. No splendor of worship can compensate for a disregard of God's moral demands. It is sheer hypocrisy to pass assumed piety as obedience to God's covenant. A congregation can be vocal in praise yet clap with blood stained hands.

God is rejecting their attempts to appear religious. Temples full of people, scent of incense, worshipers assuming the posture of prayer, liturgical detail and worship magnificent may be a spectacle, but in God's sight it has become shallow mockery.

The Father knows the intent of his children and they have "forsaken" him. They have taken lightly his command and have abandoned the covenant. To worship God is a solemn business and must be full of integrity. He knows us better than we know ourselves. God saw his chosen children with hearts of lust, greed, selfishness, injustice, and indifference. Why bring guilt and sin offerings when they were unrepentant?

To please God, one must come with humbleness, a willingness to obey, and a life to match the character of the Father. Man's reason has failed him for he thought he could lift his hands in prayer in a casual way and be accepted.

Jesus gives this same advice when he teaches us to bring our gifts to the altar and remembering aught against our brother, leave the gift, and go make peace; then return and offer our gifts (Matt 5:24).

Fathers want sincerity and integrity. To pretend a relationship that does not exist is foolish and unacceptable. Our worship and our character must coincide. To be effective, our lives must reflect his spirit and his will. Religion, without ethics, can never be acceptable. Sacrifice, without obedience, has no meaning. God is weary of such mockery and in judgment rejects their attempts to give lip service to the covenant.

Because he is so weary of their hypocrisy he will hide his eyes from them and even if they offer "many prayers" he will not listen. This is how rejected God feels at the response of his children. It is a terrible thing to feel the negative response from those you love.

The Father's Mercy: Isaiah 1:16-20

Isaiah is lost in wonder at the patience of God with Israel. Typical of the father's love, a plea is made for a change of heart and behavior. They are urged to stop doing wrong and to learn how to do right. A complete washing is needed so they can be clean. The hope for a change of heart is always the hope of a parent whose children have rebelled.

The justice of a holy God is matched by his mercy and love. God hasn't given up yet. He has left a remnant (survivors) and his divine purpose will not be frustrated. There will be those who will be spared to renew the covenant and to build anew.

What attitudes would please God? He is a holy and righteous father who wants justice done, the oppressed encouraged, the fatherless defended and the widow protected. His covenant included these precepts and his expectations for his children included their obedient response. God hasn't changed nor has his sense of righteousness.

He calls for his people to put on their thinking cap and to reason with him. Let us state the case to each other and understand fully. Faith and reason are called for in this showdown. God can be a deliverer and sins can be forgiven. However, it requires a penitent response from the child. God's promise of forgiveness is conditionally available. Forgiveness is always a divine possibility, but it requires the sinner to wake up, see what he has done or neglected to do, and confess with a repentant heart his mistakes. We do have a chance to be forgiven and to live with the Father in a new covenant.

Isaiah is not making this an unconditional promise as many evangelists have suggested. God is not mocked; nor does he take our sinfulness in a light fashion. Isaiah was convinced that a dreadful reckoning awaited those who persisted in their sins. Forgiveness and prosperity would be the reward of those who were willingly obedient to the word of the Lord.

The traditional view and use of verse 18 as a gracious invitation to partake of God's mercy needs to be altered. God does not look with favor on the petition of one who continues to sin against him. It is unreasonable to believe God is going to forgive and forget if we continue to live as we have in the past. Later Isaiah would say, "Let the wicked forsake their way, and the unrighteous their thoughts" (55:7).

So God's ability to make scarlet sins white is a possibility, but it is conditional upon man's response. Thus we play a part in the salvation plot. We must be willing and obedient to follow our father's advice. Repentance, here symbolized as washing and cleansing, is absolutely necessary before God can forgive and restore us.

In the New Testament we have many assurances of divine mercy. God has a love that goes after the lost. He wants everyone to be found, forgiven, and restored. This is a father's concern for his children. But such mercy and grace is always conditional. We need to be reasonable in our expectations and recognize that the child must be responsive, seek forgiveness, and be obedient to the Father's will. When we are "willing" good things can happen. But we must understand "grace" is conditional. We see a new note in the covenant promise, "if," and this expectation requires a change of attitude and relationship with other people.

God wants to be compassionate and wants to extend forgiveness and mercy. He wants to restore his children and deliver them. The prophet makes clear the condition: cleanse and wash yourselves, and learn to do right.

The Choice

An ultimatum is delivered: "for the mouth of the LORD has spoken" (1:20). Repent or be destroyed. It is an awesome conclusion, a death notice to the accused. If you go on rebelling, then God is going to let you die and be devoured by the sword.

Isaiah confronts his people with the power of individual choice. The Father awaits their decision. He offers the alternatives: forgiveness and a chance to live, or a death notice for those who continue in their sinfulness. Unrepentant sin will cost the child, but one who decides to allow God to be his teacher and guide will discover the depth of a father's love.

Jesus tells the parable of a prodigal son (Luke 15:11-31) who interrupts his relationship with a demand for his inheritance. This son squandered his wealth in wild living and finally ended up as a hired servant, feeding pigs. He was broke, hungry, and miserable. It was then "that he came to himself" and reasoned his situation. Humbly, he decided to return to his father's house and to ask for forgiveness. From "give me" to "make me" is the big step that qualifies one to appear before the father for forgiveness and mercy. The ending of the story portrays a father's delight and response to a prodigal son.

We have a hard time seeing ourselves as "prodigals." We go through the rituals of worship, thinking God is pleased with our meaningless offerings. Oh, that we could come to "our senses" and humbly ask for the father "to make us servants" in his Kingdom. He stands ready, able, and patiently waits for us to "come to our senses" and to realize that our sin is against God.

The prophet helps us to shift the problematic distance between the Lord's mind and our mind. The issue is not ideas but moral activity, not ignorance of God's master plan, but a "forsaking of our foolish ways and turning towards God's kind of righteousness."

Chapter Three
Learning War...
Making Peace
Isaiah 2:1-5

by Peggy A. Haymes
Associate Minister
College Park Baptist Church
Greensboro, North Carolina

More or less, the play stayed the same. With only a few
variations in plot, the actors changed. By their strength and
their skill, players emerged from the shadows to take center
stage. And although it sometimes seemed as if they could go
on forever, sooner or later their fierce power started to fade
and their strength slipped away.

Sooner or later their glory lost its shine, becoming as
tattered as a program pressed into a scrapbook. Sooner or later
a new group of players would emerge, and those who had once
shone so brightly now found themselves waiting and watching
in the wings, out of the spotlight.

So it was on the political stage in the days of Isaiah. It
was a time of the rising and falling of kingdoms. It was a time
of successful conquests and failed revolutions. Once again, the
balance of power in that part of the world was changing.

For countries like Judah who were caught in the middle of
the shifting political winds, it was an anxious time. Yesterday's
alliances could not promise tomorrow's security. It was a
dangerous time as leaders gambled their fates on who would
win and who would lose, lining up behind rulers or rebels. It

was a time of political pulse-taking, of expedient alliances and pragmatic choices.

Into such a time came the prophet Isaiah, speaking a revolutionary word, painting a radical vision. When the king of Israel had to make a choice of whether to cast his lot with the ruling Assyrians or to take his chances with those rebelling against Assyrian rule, Isaiah counseled "none of the above." Be patient and wait upon God, he argued. Trust only in God.

But the king was a pragmatic fellow, and being of a practical bent, he knew that treaties were more tangible than a prophet's promises. He appealed to Assyria for help against the rebels, and in return Judah fell under the domination of Assyria.

His advice unheeded, Isaiah withdrew from public life. But he continued to speak a radical word and to weave a strange vision. He spoke of a different kind of a day, a day when the nations would flock to Jerusalem not to conquer, but to but to seek the Word of God. Nations would gather at the Temple, not to offer sacrifice but to learn the ways of God.

Not only that, but they would re-forge and reshape their swords, making them into plowshares. They would turn their spears into pruning hooks. The disputes of nations would not be decided by soldiers and kings, but by the Lord God. No longer would the nations learn war, but would live in peace.

It was an incredible vision for Isaiah's time, with its wars and rumors of war. It is a strange and wondrous vision for our time—a military march transformed into a pastoral symphony. The weapons of destruction become the tools of agriculture. It is a vision of a peace deeper and more lasting than armed stand-offs and uneasy truces.

But that's all that it is—a vision. For it has been thousands of years since Isaiah's day, and we seem no closer to it. There are always wars somewhere or another, and if history teaches us anything, there always will be wars. At least until Jesus comes. That's just the way that life is.

Or is it? Isn't it interesting that the prophet speaks of nations "learning war." And perhaps it is that the art of war must be learned. Not merely the military maneuvers, for it's much more basic than that. We have to be taught, from the very beginning, the most basic lessons.

We learn very early that it's us against them. We learn to hate other peoples and other countries, or at least to be suspicious of them. We have to learn that no matter the issue, we are right and they, whoever "they" happen to be, are wrong. We learn to walk, but we also learn to hit and to hate.

If you want to see an illustration of the power of the lessons that we absorb from the world around us, consider the case of the Soviet Union. A few short years ago they were considered to be "the evil empire." At all costs, at any costs, we had to stay one step ahead of them. Working with them was out of the question. But now we enlist them to stand with us, to be our allies in preserving the order of things, and there is little talk of evil empires. We have to be taught whom to hate and whom to cheer.

It's true on a global scale. But it is also true on an individual scale as we fight our thousands of petty wars with one another. We have to learn who is "in" and who is "out" and how to tell the difference. We have to learn the icy stares and subtle put-downs and words that twist like knives. We have to learn how to build our walls and fortify our defenses, whom to let in and whom to exclude, who is a stranger and who is a friend. There is so much to learn.

But the old song says, "I'm gonna lay down my sword and shield down by the riverside. Ain't gonna study war no more." And the prophet Isaiah says, "Nation shall not lift up sword against nation, neither shall they learn war any more" (Isa 2:4b). And Jesus the Christ says, "Blessed are the peacemakers, for they will be called children of God" (Matt 5:9).

In the end, it comes down to a question of trust. In whom, or in what, shall we trust? Our coins proclaim, "In God We Trust", but you and I know that it's not true. For if you look at what we do with those coins, it becomes clear that we believe that our security is in bombs and guns, missiles and tanks. Our trust is in the most technologically sophisticated and gee-whiz, newfangled weapons.

But such security is no security at all. We now have a

generation of adults who have lived their whole lives under the mushroom-shaped shadow of the Bomb. Their lives have been buffeted by the never ending questions—who has it, who is developing it, and the most frightening question of all, who will use it? In the midst of all the warheads, where is the security?

We cheer the latest weapon developments, only to find that they will not work in the jungle or in the desert, or on urban battlefields. Billion dollar systems turn out to be fatally flawed, or prematurely obsolete. All the while families go without the basics of food and shelter, because there is no more money for affordable housing or emergency relief. All the while people suffer untreated illnesses because there is no more money for health care. All the while our schools hold bake sales and trim budgets and cut back to bare bones necessities, because there is no more money for educating the next generation. In such a system, where is the security?

And it is no different for us in our everyday lives. We buy handguns to make our homes secure, only to have our children kill each other with them. We buy more and more sophisticated alarm systems for our homes and our cars. By all means, we ought to be the most secure people ever to live on this planet. But somehow, it's never enough. The locks are never big enough and the alarms are never loud enough. Where is the security? To whom shall we look? In whom shall we trust?

The questions bring a chuckle and a far-off stare, as the prophet leans back in his chair. He shakes his head and wonders when they will ever learn. Assyrians are now the stuff of history books, along with a hundred other kingdoms that arose only to fall. Not to mention the ones never remembered at all. They're no more than dust now.

Only One has endured. Only One who was before time and will be at the end of time. Only One whose power will not fail and whose glory will not fade. "Where is the security?," Isaiah repeats the question softly. "Only in this One. Only in God".

So come, let us go to the house of God. Let us learn the ways of our Lord. Let us learn the ways of peace as earnestly as we have learned the ways of war. Let us learn to see what unites us as clearly as we have seen what divides us. Let us spend as much time and energy and money learning the things that make for peace as making the things of war.

For kingdoms are rising and falling. It is a time of political pulse-taking and pragmatic alliances. It is a time of questions and of choices, a time to make decisions.

So let *us* choose for peace. Not because we are little Pollyannas, believing only in sunshine. Sometimes the clouds are much too dark for that. Let us choose for peace, but not because it is the easy way out. To the contrary, it may be the hardest road of all, requiring both great courage and great commitment. When a people are primed for war, peacemaking is not popular.

Let us choose for peace, not because it will make us look good. Indeed, it may make us look a little foolish, but we would not be the first to risk becoming fools for the sake of Christ.

Let us make peace, not because the task is easy and easily accomplished. To the contrary, it is daunting and at times, seemingly impossible. We may be forgiven an occasional dose of cynicism, for the wars to end all wars haven't. So who are we to make a difference?

The task may seem impossible, and yet deep down we know that there is more power in a single act of reconciliation than in our bombs and missiles, for they bring only death, and reconciliation brings life. And we serve a Lord who has shown by his life that, in the end, death cannot win. Therefore, no act of love is futile. We are never without hope. And we are never alone.

Isaiah envisioned a new day. With the Christ, that new day has begun. The kingdom is not yet come, but it has broken into our lives and we are called to live by its peculiar ways. The kingdom has come and is coming, and in such a kingdom plowshares are infinitely more valuable than swords. Pruning hooks are preferred to spears.

So, let us choose for peace and learn its ways, simply because we are the people of God, called to walk in God's path.

Called to speak the good news of the Prince of Peace. Called to live out that good news in our communities and in our world.

Blessed are the peacemakers, for they may be called the children of God. May it be so with us, O Lord. May it be so with us.

Chapter Four
Saying It With a Song
Isaiah 5:1-7

by Marion D. Lark
Senior Minister, First Baptist Church Henderson,
North Carolina

"What cannot be explained can be addressed, at least in song," said Martin Marty.[1] Maybe that was the thinking of this singer of Israel who goes by the name of Isaiah. The Isaiah who sings a love song concerning his friend's vineyard.

Why is it that some things can be addressed in song but not explained? Are there not sufficient words to explain? Is there fear the hearers will not understand? Is the subject too sensitive, too hot to handle? Maybe the answer is all of the above or none of the above. It is a fact, however, that in every age songs have been used to address individuals and nations. Songs that inspire or rebuke or tell a story or make a point. Songs like Negro spirituals which voice the agony of slavery or songs of protest which question the reason for war. And yes, love songs of every variety and vintage which spin tales of one's beloved whose faithfulness is acclaimed or called into question.

It does seem some things are more readily addressed in song than explained in words. That is what Isaiah chose to do when on some festival occasion, he sang what we know as "The Song of the Vineyard."

The opening stanza of this song tells of a vineyard on a fertile hill. But one cannot listen long without such words as plan and preparation coming to mind. Words that are indicative of *design*. It is no accident this hillside is covered with

43

grapevines. The owner of that plot had cleared it of rocks, plowed it deeply, planted it carefully, built a tower to protect it, prepared a vat for making wine, then looked intently for the vineyard to produce quality fruit. Did you note the verbs of action? Hear them again. The owner *cleared, plowed, planted, built, made,* and *looked.* That vineyard was there not by happenstance, but by design and at considerable expense.

While spending time in Europe my wife and I had opportunity to take a cruise down Germany's Rhine River. That swift-moving stream carried us past ancient castles and lovely forests. But even these were hardly a match for the beauty of vineyards we saw planted at steep angles on the hillside above the river valley. We were impressed with how much planning and preparation must have gone into those vineyards. And we could only imagine just how much the owners expected from them.

Design and preparation, intention and expectation are dominant notes in this first stanza of Isaiah's love song. In spite of that owner's careful design, a certain disappointment emerges. Grapes are produced but they are bitter, not sweet. They cannot be used. The love song which began on a note of creative enthusiasm now, in the second stanza, sounds this note of painful *disappointment,* "but it yielded wild grapes" (5:2).

Through the hurt of disappointment comes the owner's lament, "What more was there to do for my vineyard that I have not done in it?" (5:4). From this rhetorical question these first hearers learn what the owner will do to his vineyard. He will remove its hedge, break down its protective wall, and lay waste its vines. Did you note these words? Hear them again. The owner will *remove, break down,* and *lay waste.* Just as surely as he designed this vineyard and then experienced disappointment with its bitter fruit, now he will undo what he had done and *distance* himself from it. In essence he will leave it alone; he will abandon it.[2] Was this poignant word in the third stanza meant to elicit sympathy for the owner? Were these hearers so enthralled with the immediate situation they were unaware of an impending application?

This love song is not just about a vineyard on some Judean hillside. But *we,* the readers, have known that all along.

We know it is a story, a parable, which tells about a relationship between God and his people. And this ancient singer did not keep his audience guessing long either. Right away with a crescendo born of concern the singer reveals that the Lord is the Owner. Israel is the vineyard. She has failed to produce usable fruit. God is disappointed. He will leave her alone. He will judge Israel.

Look again at the elements of design, disappointment and distancing found in this story. Did not God by *design* call these wandering people out of exile in Egypt? Hosea's "love song" also sounds this note. The Lord says, "When Israel was a child, I loved him and out of Egypt I called my son" (Hosea 11:1). Soon this same prophet echoes the pathos of divine *disappointment*. "The more I called them, the more they went from me" (Hosea 11:2). Concerning the song from Isaiah, Delores S. Williams observes that it is full of proper and good intentions about the vineyard beginnings. But sometimes things go wrong and the harvest is disappointing.[3] It hardly needs saying that in this "Song of the Vineyard" divine disappointment comes on the heels of unfulfilled expectations. In terms of justice and righteousness the Chosen People fail to produce. Speaking for God the ancient singer said: "He expected justice, but saw bloodshed; righteousness, but heard a cry!" (5:7).

Suddenly, notes of pathos are everywhere. Now it seems that what has been addressed in song also has been explained. Explained all too clearly for those hearing it.

Design, disappointment, and now the note that God will *distance* himself from Israel. Yet, in the larger context of this prophet's message are we not given to understand these people could hardly believe what they were hearing? How could God distance himself from them? They were his beloved, blessed with privilege and protection. It seems as if they were saying to Isaiah, "You do not know whereof you speak. Our God will take care of us, no matter what." My friend and spiritual mentor Ed Laffman says these people claimed they were inviolable because they were the chosen of God. With his reckless talk of God abandoning them as some angry owner did with a vineyard, might they have accused Isaiah of heresy? In truth was not the sandal on the other foot? Did not the heresy lie in the fact that Israel expected protection and blessing from God, but failed to practice justice and righteousness for God?[4] Like a fugue in a Bach composition the covenant theme was ever recurring, a theme which revealed mutual expectations and promises between God and Israel. In light of this covenant Israel knew what to expect from God. How could she not know what God expected from her.

Years ago I heard Kenneth Chafin tell of accompanying some fellow students to see one of Shakespeare's plays. The drama was a class assignment, but Chafin was not in the class and only went along to be with friends. He was not familiar with the play and kept asking his friends what was going on. They told him to be quiet and not to interrupt. He said he soon came to the conclusion that while he did not know what was going on, his fellow students taking the course knew from the beginning what to expect and how it would end.

Because of the covenant Israel knew from the beginning what God expected. Yet she presumed this loving God would, if necessary, alter his laws on her behalf. Surely he would not "break down the walls of protection" around her. This presumptuous denial of a revealed truth, this unilateral dissent from an agreement made is but further evidence that Israel came to misunderstand her role or chose to ignore it. Now in essence Israel has the shock of hearing God say to her what Nathan said to King David, "You are the one." Genuine love does confront. When necessary, accusations are made and guilt disclosed. Israel had been addressed in song and now the notes of judgment were sounding everywhere.

It has been stated that Isaiah's song is not just a ballad about a vineyard in ancient Israel. Nor is it only about an ancient people who did not live up to God's expectations. It is a story whose truth is both timeless and timely.

Paul Scherer tells of a drama he read about which takes place in a theater filled with people waiting for the curtain to go up. When it does rise another set is disclosed with yet another curtain rising, then another. The original audience, now a bit uneasy, wonders if it, too, is on stage.[5] The people of God today are on stage, participants in a divine-human drama. When listening to the first stanza of Isaiah's song we of the church are relaxed because, like Israel, we count ourselves as part of God's design. We point to ourselves and quote with approval Jesus' words, "You did not choose me but I chose you. And I appointed you to go and bear fruit . . ." (John 15:16). Some even declare our land is a "Christian nation"; otherwise, they ask, how could we be so blessed? And of the Southern Baptist Convention many have seriously claimed it to be "God's last and only hope." Little wonder that such interpretations of the divine design make for ease in Zion.

But how willing are we to admit that our produce of sometimes bitter fruit has brought *disappointment* to the heart of our Beloved? Reasons given to explain that divine disappointment would be numerous. Scorekeepers of wrong could compose a catalogue of sins as did Isaiah in those words which follow his song. Sins not unlike those he listed such as greed, drunkenness, bribery, moral indiscretion, blasphemy, and injustice. Honesty would require that to these we add dishonesty, prejudice, indifference, selfishness, strife, war and murder. And that is just the beginning! Yet, it was not so much the *sins* of Israel that elicited divine disappointment as it was the sin of *we can do what we want because God is on our side.* Thus presuming to live for God without listening to God Israel quickly moved toward replacing the great God of justice and righteousness with the lesser gods of symbols, rituals and institutions.

Elizabeth Achtemeier warns that, "Apart from God's continuing guidance we do not know how to live . . . . And so in love he gives us direction to point the way to wholeness, life and joy. Sometimes, of course, we do not like the directions."[6] As with Israel, so many in the church today not liking the directions which come from divine wisdom, or simply taking the road requiring less discipline, or presuming that, after all, God prefers mega-churches, authoritarian leaders, solemn assemblies, noisy songs, and popular programs, seek to live for him without carefully listening to him. Then has God distanced himself from the institutional church because ritual has replaced righteousness, because institutions and programs have become all too often the golden calf of another day, and because leaders who need to be led by God are more interested in achieving power and popularity among their peers and parishioner?

Frederick Buechner says it happened with Israel.

> "We are delivered" they said in their Temple while it was still in business. They had been delivered at the Exodus and many a time since. They had left behind them in Egypt the worst bondage of all which was bondage to themselves. They had been shown the way to get the hell out, but they were still in hell because by letting their faith become mainly a matter of ritual and busyness inside the Temple and by living their lives outside the Temple as though there was no God at all, hell was what they had made for themselves and within themselves.[7]

Buechner goes on to say the people of Israel are now on their own.

All over Europe in small villages and large cities cathedrals can be seen with their majestic spires pointing toward the heavens. Many of these buildings which once were alive with communities of faith evidenced by enthusiastic congregations, joyful worship, and service for Christ in the world are now little more than museums or tourist attractions for international visitors. The buildings are as stately as ever, in many the ritual is still practiced, but to some observers it appears the Spirit which fosters life and love, freedom and force, justice and righteousness, growth and grace is absent. But can we point one finger at the church in Europe without at the same time making a three-fold indictment on many institutional aspects of Christianity on this side of the Atlantic?

Moreover, has God distanced himself from a people called Southern Baptists? Before attempting to answer that question, can it not be affirmed that in some measure the hand of God was in the design of this denomination. And that unlike the vineyard of which Isaiah sang this Baptist vineyard did, for a while anyway, produce "good grapes" such as biblical authority, confessions of faith, cooperative missions, separation of church and state, the priesthood of the believer, the autonomy of the local church, intellectual integrity, genuine worship, authentic evangelism and responsible ministry from its "choice vines" carefully planted and nurtured.

The intervening years though, at least in the minds of many, have brought about a harvest of "bitter fruit" from this vineyard which carries the Baptist label. "Bitter fruit" such as biblical inerrancy, creedal statements, theological indoctrination, civil religion, convention hierarchy, and pastoral authority. Does not such a bitter harvest result in painful disappointment?

The more critical question is whether or not God has distanced himself from his people in the Southern Baptist vineyard? Who among us has even the right to ask such a question, much less make an implication? Does it not smack of heresy, if not blasphemy? Moreover, who among us has the wisdom even to imagine what God would think about anything so institutional? Yet, what if through our controversy we have failed to do justice and righteousness and replaced them with in-fighting and self-interest, thus treading upon the once choice vines of this vineyard? Then does this "song" about the institutional church and a denominational organization end as Isaiah's song did with a discordant note that the owner has distanced himself?

In telling this story Isaiah leaves no doubt that the owner will prevail. What he says he will do to his vineyard will be done. Often, one who prevails experiences a sense of triumph at having the last word. But when this singer addresses the people of Israel in song and identifies them as the vineyard which will be removed, is there even a hint that the Owner, God, is ready to sound a note of victory because he has prevailed?

Perhaps we get a clue to such an inquiry from an experience Robert McAfee Brown had while listening to Ralph Vaughan Williams' musical work, *Sancta Civita*, for multiple chorus and orchestra. This work tells of the fall of Babylon and the ultimate triumph of the Holy City. Brown expected Williams would use trumpets, timpani and cymbals to provide a crescendo of victorious celebration. The composer does not do that. Instead of the chorus being *fortissimo*, it is *pianissimo*. Brown says there is no ringing celebration because "there are too many wounded, too many dead, there has been too much devastation."[8]

Isaiah's "Song of the Vineyard" which began on a gentle

note with an apparently innocuous theme, soon crashed in upon its hearers conveying that many would be wounded and a quiet devastation would abound in a once beautiful vineyard. It happened. But there is not ever a hint that the Owner received satisfaction because he had prevailed, or that such circumstances merited any kind of celebration. As with Israel, so with much of the institutional church in general and the Southern Baptist Convention in particular, there is much devastation and many are wounded. Surely, whatever sound is heard from the Owner is marked *pianissimo*.

It may be, however, that in those muted tones a note of hope can be heard. What if that hope lies within rather than without? What if the Transcendent Being becomes the indwelling Spirit? What if God who refuses to be a co-dependent to spiritual dysfunction, whether for ancient Israel, the contemporary church, or a convention, continues to distance himself so that his people *have* to assume responsibility for their world?

We of the church like to sing the spiritual, "He's Got the Whole World in His Hands." Suppose this time the Lord sings to his beloved and the words are these, "You've Got the Whole World in Your Hands." That is, you have another chance to produce fruits of justice and righteousness. What if our faith affirmation, "We believe in God" should be turned the other way so that God says to us, "I believe in you?" Would not this be a new sign of his grace? The grace of another chance? To use language of the land, perhaps the ground of whatever vineyard we claim to be, church or convention, will have to lie fallow for a time. Martin Marty says that fallow land though unseeded and unproductive represents a kind of hope.[9] And, in addition, does not this time of rest allow the natural order to heal, replenish and restore the land?

Might not the church or a convention in repentance lie fallow until such time as God's laborers finally assume responsibility for the land, plow it thoroughly, redesign the layout, carefully plant the seed and wait expectantly for fruit with which to make new wine worthy of the Kingdom label?

Dare we take hope in the words of another who called himself Isaiah?

> Therefore the LORD waits to be gracious to you; therefore he will rise up to show mercy to you. For the LORD is a God of justice; blessed are all those who wait for him. Though the LORD may give you the bread of adversity and the water of affliction, yet your Teacher will not hide himself anymore, but your eyes shall see your Teacher. And when you turn to the right or when you turn to the left, your ears shall hear a word behind you, saying, "This is the way; walk in it" (Isa 30:18,20-21).

Is not this music to our ears and a song for our hearts?

Notes

[1] Martin E. Marty, *A Cry of Absence* (San Francisco: Harper and Row, Publishers, 1983), p.145.

[2] Page H. Kelly, "Isaiah," *The Broadman Bible Commentary*, vol. 5. Clifton J. Allen, Ed. (Nashville: Broadman Press, 1971), p. 204.

[3] Delores S. Williams, "The Salvation of Growth," *The Christian Century* (October, 1990): 899.

[4] Conversation with Reverend Edward Laffman.

[5] Paul Scherer, *The Word God Sent* (New York: Harper and Row, Publishers, 1965), p. 133.

[6] Elizabeth Achtemeir, "Renewed Appreciation For an Unchanging Story," *The Christian Century* (June 13-20, 1990): 597.

[7] Frederick Buechner, *A Room Called Remember* (San Francisco: Harper and Row, Publishers, 1984), p. 118.

[8] Robert McAfee Brown, *Creative Dislocation—The Movement of Grace* (Nashville: Abingdon Press, 1980), pp. 25-26.

[9] Martin E. Marty, *A Cry of Absence* (San Francisco: Harper and Row, Publisher, 1983), p.151.

Chapter Five
Isaiah:
I Saw the Lord
Isaiah 6:1-8

by W. Randall Lolley
Pastor, First Baptist Church
Greensboro, North Carolina

The last half of the Old Testament records the works of 15 prophets (plus the book of Daniel). The writing prophets, as they are sometimes called, flourished during the three-century span from mid eighth to mid fifth century B.C. These books are not found in any chronological order. Rather they are arranged to some extent on the basis of length. Fully two-thirds of the material in these prophetic books is found in the first three—Isaiah, Jeremiah and Ezekiel.

These three do appear in chronological sequence. Isaiah deals with the period of Assyrian ascendancy as a world power. Jeremiah deals with the period of Babylonian ascendancy. And Ezekiel is a prophet of the exile in Babylon.

Perhaps the best known and most loved of all the prophets is Isaiah. It is from that matchless book that we now share some insights.

All we know of Isaiah is provided autobiographically in the book that bears his name. His father was Amoz. So far as we know he is mentioned only this once in the Old Testament. So, who he was we can only conjecture.

There is a rabbinic tradition that Amoz, Isaiah's father, was a brother of Amaziah, Judah's former king, and Uzziah's father. If this were so, then Isaiah would be a member of the royal family and a first cousin of King Uzziah, whose death marked the date of Isaiah's call to be a prophet.

Students of scripture judge from Isaiah's writing style that he did indeed belong to the upper class in Judah. If this be so, here was an aristocrat who lived and worked on behalf of the dispossessed masses in his homeland. Few men in history have ever championed more eloquently the cause of the poor and disfranchised. Like most of the prophets Isaiah was radical, insisting that ritual was no substitute for true religion in Judah or anywhere else.

The general period in which Isaiah carried out his prophetic mission is given in the first verse of the book: "The vision of Isaiah . . . which he saw concerning Judah in the days of Uzziah, Jotham, Ahaz, and Hezekiah, kings of Judah" (1:1). Remember that by this time in Hebrew history, Solomon's Empire had been divided in both land and leadership. Israel in the North had her kings. Judah, in the South, had her kings.

Isaiah's work was directed in the main to the Southern Kingdom of Judah. His life extended through the reigns of four kings: Uzziah, Jotham, Ahaz, Hezekiah.

Since Uzziah came to Judah's throne in 783 B.C. and Hezekiah died in 742 B.C., this makes Isaiah a man of the eighth century B.C. For the actual year of the beginning of his prophetic career, we turn to the sixth chapter. It begins like this: "In the year that King Uzziah died, I saw the Lord, sitting on a throne, high and lofty" (6:1).

Uzziah died in 742 B.C., a time when Judah's power and prosperity were at their peak. Isaiah could not have been much more than twenty years old when he experienced the vision which launched his prophetic career. We might expect the record of his call to come in the first rather than the sixth chapter. But what we have here is a prophetic remembrance, the beginnings looked back upon from well into the journey.

Success came hard for a prophet in eighth century Judah. Not everyone came running to join his crusade. Isaiah's call had not ended; it had begun his struggle against overwhelming odds. So, well into the journey he sought to vindicate the results (or lack of them) to his own heart. Thus, he harkened back to the beginnings.

You see, ministry does not chronicle by time but by experience. So this sixth chapter is a cardinal event, an experience often reflected upon and frequently referred to during Isaiah's lifetime. Let's review it for some insights which apply to us here and now.

Isaiah's sixth chapter is autobiographical. It is the most detailed and vivid account in scripture of the making of a prophet. The miracle is that the prophet was fashioned out of an ordinary human being, a mere man who had a soul-shaking experience of the reality of God.

"In the year that King Uzziah died, I saw the Lord . . . . " This strange sentence becomes even more intense when you consider that his King was dead, his countrymen were mourning, his flag was at half-mast, and his nation ready to grasp at straws.

See this young man in the Jerusalem temple, the one Solomon had built. See him well; let him teach us some things we can do, in times like these when the land wipes its brow, mops up its mess, gasps for breath, and grapples on the brink of a national nervous breakdown. When the flag flies at half-mast, and the country has a fever—what then? Isaiah tells us.

The first thing Isaiah does is survey the field for evidences of God. Uzziah had been a good King in Judah. His death had smashed the citizenry. He had ruled over forty years; sixteen of which were from his isolated infirmary where he had suffered leprosy. Such a long tenure would be a span of time that would encompass the presidential terms of Truman, Eisenhower, Kennedy, Johnson, Nixon, Ford, Carter, Reagan, and Bush. The Empire was at a peak it had not known since Solomon.

Uzziah conquered the Philistines toward the Mediterranean, the Ammorites to the South, and the Edomites in the wastes of Arabia. He substantially improved the walls of Jerusalem, his capital city. He built a port city on the gulf of Akabah and a number of storage cities in the southern deserts. He championed agriculture and taught his countrymen how to improve the strains of their sheep, horses, and cattle. He increased his nation's water supply by digging many wells and developing a system of aqueducts. His reign had been punctuated by both peace and prosperity. But now King Uzziah was dead. The people were smashed; especially the young felt a light had gone out.

And for young Isaiah it was a time for soul searching. Isaiah had loved Uzziah. Chances are, they were cousins. In all likelihood, his king had appointed Isaiah as a member of the court. He had watched the affairs of state unfold from the inside. Now the news of his monarch's death fell with a thud upon him. In Judah, too, there had been "a time of lightning and a day of drums."

See young Isaiah! First, he went to the *palace* where he recalled the stirring speeches and wise decisions he had come to expect from his king. Now the palace was beautiful, but empty. The throne room was gilded but untenanted. Next he visited the *infirmary* when for months his king had battled the dreaded leprosy. Here the fearsome disease had won the long battle and robbed the nation of its leader. Then he visited the *cemetery* where they had left the remains of his friend. Even here the beauty of the funeral memories, in their coldness, left him numb. The king was dead! The nation mourned. Young Isaiah was smashed.

Then Isaiah did a most significant thing. He returned to the *temple*, to the very place where the priests had intoned their funeral dirges for the king. He recalled all the sights and sounds which ended in a requiem. He knew too that at this very place shortly thereafter Judah would crown herself a new king.

And then it happened! But let him tell us in his own words:

> In the year that King Uzziah died, I saw the Lord sitting on a throne, high and lofty, and the hem of his robe filled the temple. Seraphs were in attendance above him . . . . And one called to another and said, "Holy, Holy, Holy is the LORD of hosts, the whole earth is full of his glory." The pivots on the thresholds shook at the voices of those who called, and the house was filled with smoke (6:1-4).

The moment of truth in that experience breaks through. The king who was gone was replaced by a vision of a King who was always there—always had been—always would be. In the aftermath, Isaiah saw God, and sensed something steady over all the wreckage.

Now that is what a man of faith can do when his situation gets desperate. When the flag will not fly and the country hurts, a man of faith can survey the field for evidences of God. But I warn you, it is a difficult discipline. It is far easier to become frightened, frustrated, suspicious, and sick. For when something precious in the nation dies, it is easy to conclude that God has abdicated also.

Jesus Christ, in the days of his flesh, had a word about precisely this crisis: "Blessed are the pure in heart, for they shall see God" (Matt 5:8). There is a vision born of a pure heart. It depends totally upon the right equipment for seeing. Eyes cannot do it. Mind cannot do it. It is a vision of the heart. Such a vision of God does not stem from standard human equipment.

It is the vision of proper worship. It is the vision of confrontation, encounter, exposure. One who does not worship right can hardly expect to see God at work in this troubled world. It is no wonder then that so many now see only dictators, terrorists, drug lords, subversives, people plotting an overthrow. Hear young Isaiah at the toughest time in his life— "I saw the Lord."

Isaiah saw the Lord *in correct perspective* ("high, holy, enthroned"). The God he saw was one worthy to be worshiped. God was no superhuman big brother who could be maneuvered or manipulated. God was no toothless, clawless lion of Judah.

Isaiah was no longer restricted by having no one larger or nothing stronger than himself upon whom to depend. The God who came to him was larger than the temple. His train filled it. The smoke of his holy presence cascaded all out-of-doors. The whole earth was full of God's glory.

Isaiah saw the Lord *in correct proximity* ("train filled the temple"). Imagine that, the Lord God of Judah (high, holy, enthroned) was yet in the very place where Isaiah was. In the rough and tumble of his right now experience, he sensed the awesome presence of God. This was no absentee deity, a thousand layers of clouds away. Here was God in his world—

not as a tourist seeing the sights, but as a redeemer putting things right.

Isaiah found that it is not the office of faith to seek out a God who is hard to find. Rather it is the task of faith to be found by a God who constantly seeks God's own. It is not terribly difficult to believe in God, unless we try to define God.

Isaiah saw the Lord *in correct proportion and power* ("At his voice the foundations of the threshold shook"). This is not the power of a doting grandfather deity who will shut one eye and approve us just any old way. Here is the tough and persistent power of redemptive love (*ḥesed* the Old Testament calls it). God's is not so much the power to blast humankind into eternity, as it is the power to bring eternity into humankind.

"I Saw the Lord. . . . ." That confession of Isaiah at the front door of his mission, raises a good question. When our situation becomes desperate, what do we see? Our answer to that question says volumes about the quality of our worship.

Have you noticed? Our Sunday services at 11:00 A.M. have come to be called "preaching services" rather than "worship services." This means that if for some reason we do not resonate with the preacher, then we do not resonate with the worship.

Now, I am a preacher and deeply appreciate the place of the sermon in worship. But suppose you do not like the sermon? Suppose you do not appreciate the preacher? Is the hour wasted?

Note this well! Isaiah does not say, "In the year that Uzziah died, I heard a sermon with which I totally agreed." Rather he said, "I saw the Lord." As devastating as it is to the preacher in me, there was no sermon preached in the temple that day.

Yet worship happened—gloriously happened! A young man ceased to be a spectator in the temple that day. He became a participant. When your situation becomes desperate, what do you see?

Andrew Johnson, Vice President, was in a New York hotel when Abraham Lincoln was assassinated. He was thirty-four years old and faced with the awesome responsibility of becoming President. The crowd outside his hotel was devastated, angry, restless, thirsty for revenge.

When Johnson finally came out to make a statement, he chose a biblical text as part of his witness: "'Justice and judgment are the habitation of God's throne. Mercy and truth shall go before God's face.' My fellow citizens, God reigns, the Republic yet lives, and life will go on." In the nation's darkest hour, young Johnson saw God.

Yet, faithless little human beings live their lives out as if God were never there, and as if it does not matter whether God is. But God is there and here; and it does matter. It matters greatly! It remains for us in faith to see God and lead others to know of God's presence for those who have the vision for it.

Remember the experience of the two men exploring the same strange new world of outer space? Russian Cosmonaut Yuri Gagarin said that while he was circling the world in space he did not see anything to make him believe in God. American astronaut John Glenn said, the God to whom he addresses his prayers is not so small that he would expect to see him on a few clouds or even on the mighty oceans of space.

It is more than a point of view. It is a matter of being equipped to see. "Blessed are the pure in heart, for they shall see God" (Matt 5:8.). In proper perspective, proximity, power, it remains for faith to see God.

Isaiah shows us one thing more, that a person in crisis can do. *He identifies with his countrymen's sickness and dedicates himself to bringing them wholeness and health.* Again, hear the young prophet in the temple: "Then said I, 'Woe is me! For I am undone, because I am a man of unclean lips, and I dwell in the midst of a people of unclean lips'" (6:5).

When we see God aright then we correctly see ourselves! For the most part, we are content with ourselves. We seldom deal frankly in self-examination. We compare ourselves with others and persuade ourselves that we are as good or better than they—just as we are. And then something happens, something big! It shocks us out of our complacency and gives us occasion for appraisal.

All of us are in the company of the "sick of this land." Our sins have made it so. We need one and all the Great Physician and that very real redemption from ourselves, and the deliverance from the unsavory brew we always cook up when left alone in the kitchen. Here is the good news of both Isaiah and Jesus—"We are *not* left alone in the kitchen." We can each one feel the live coal from off the altar of God, and its searing, cleansing in Jesus Christ.

Remember Tess, the tragic, twisted girl created in one of Thomas Hardy's novels? Hardy left her dying amid the eerie ruins of Stonehope with a bitter word: "Justice was done and the President of the Immortals had finished his sport with Tess."

Hardy was wrong—all wrong! Heaven is not ruled by some irrational clown who in his caprice does sport with us. In our tragedy, God engages not in sport, but in deliverance. And in the process we see ourselves—unclean, undone; commissioned to minister to an unclean and undone people. So, the truth from this page snatched out of Isaiah's prophetic pilgrimage comes home to us. And here is the truth; in our crises God engages not in sport, but in deliverance! Amen.

Chapter Six
Gripped by the Certainty of God
Isaiah Chapter 6

by Rex Mason

Senior Tutor, Regent's Park College
and University Lecturer
University of Oxford, England

My Old Testament teacher, Aubrey Johnson, would tell those close to him of a remarkable experience he had as a young research student in, of all places, the Bodleian Library in Oxford. He was preparing a thesis on the influence of classical literature and ideas on the Old Testament, although this was only a time-filling ploy while he worked on his own position with regard to the Bible and his faith generally. He was reading Baudissin's massive study *Adonis Und Esmun*—not, many of us might have thought, a likely source for an almost mystical experience. But as he came to what Baudissin has to say about Yahweh as the God of LIFE, everything suddenly fell into place. He saw, in that moment, the direction of his whole life's work spread out before him—and all his subsequent writing was the working out of the plan which came to him then, sadly, never to be completed with the projected *Theology of the Bible* for which all his great monographs were but prolegomena. So seized was he by the wonder of this moment of revelation that he describes how he left his books in the Bodleian and walked for hours, possessed by the exaltation of one who has suddenly been vouchsafed a vision.

61

I mention him since it seems something of the same thing happened to Isaiah of Jerusalem. Whether or not he had his great vision of God described in chapter 6 in the temple, the revelation given to him there was to determine all his preaching, all his subsequent reactions to the successive crises and events of his crowded lifetime. Like an overture to a great operatic work, all the main themes of Isaiah's theology are to be found in germ in Chapter 6.

It is of the highest significance that it was in the year that king Uzziah died that he was gripped by the certainty of a God who reigns over all kings and nations and disposes all human history, sitting on a throne higher than that of any Judean monarch, higher even than the towering throne of the great power and despot of the day, Tiglath-pileser III, the king of Assyria. Uzziah had been on the throne of Judah for forty years. Two generations would hardly remember another king, and it had been a time of solidity, peace and prosperity. Now this great figure passes from the scene just as the dark international storm clouds are beginning to loom on the horizon with the growth and expansionist policies of the Assyrians. It is at just this time, when the comforting and familiar human landmarks are being eclipsed, that Isaiah becomes overwhelmed with the towering sense of God's sovereignty and power. It is a conviction that will inform all his preaching. Even the march of the world super-power of his day is only the working out of God's purposes in history. Assyria is no more than the tool in God's hand and, although in the arrogance of its kings, it boasts of its own great power, it will be cut down to size by the sovereign God (10: 5-19). How ridiculous, in fact, is all human pretension, pride and vaunted independence before a God who is so much greater than everything human. There is no human pride which will not be cut down to size by this God (2:11-19). How foolish is the so-called "wisdom" of the statesmen of the court who counsel seeking the shelter of a military and political alliance with a country like Egypt instead of relying on God (see 31:1-3). Instead the only proper response to God (as well perhaps as the only prudential political course) is a response to God of utter and complete trust in this power: "In returning and rest you shall be saved; in quietness and in trust shall be your strength" (30:15).

To the fearful Ahaz, quivering before the combined on-slaught of Israel and Syria, he puns on the Hebrew word "believe," from which we get our word "Amen" and which has a basic meaning of "to support." So we might try to catch the play on ideas, if not of words, in English by rendering, "If you do not lean on God, how can he support you?" (7:9, author's translation).

So Isaiah glimpses what we might term the transcendence of the sovereign God. But the vision brings so big a God to the prophet that, at the same time, he becomes conscious of his uncompromising holiness. The song of the seraphim suggests that this is the prime theme of his subjects' worship, "Holy, holy, holy is the LORD of hosts." The phrase "LORD of hosts" is used repeatedly by Isaiah. Traditionally it was associated with the idea of the power of the God who led out Israel's armies and fought their battles, and was a title particularly associated with the ark of the covenant (I Sam 4:4), itself a war palladium (Num 10:33-36). Yet, it seems, Yahweh's power and might are, for Isaiah, demonstrated as much in his holiness as by his military prowess.

In what, then, does this holiness consist? It is difficult for us to realize that the term "holiness" (Hebrew *qadosh*) origi-nally had little to do with ethical righteousness. It stood for "the other," the "sacred," as opposed to the "profane" (Latin *pro-fanus*, "before," or "outside the temple"). It is extraordinary to recall that, amongst Israel's neighbors, sacred prostitutes who functioned in the sanctuary cult could be known as "holy men" and "holy women." It is entirely due to the insight and vision of prophets like Isaiah that it came to be seen that Yahweh's "otherness" consisted exactly in his complete ethical righteousness. That is why, in the face of this vision, Isaiah becomes overwhelmed with a deep sense of his own sin and that of the people he is representing: "Woe is me! I am lost, for I am a man of unclean lips, and I dwell among a people of unclean lips."

Or, as Isaiah 5:16 has it, "But the LORD of hosts is exalted

by justice, and the Holy God shows himself holy by righteousness." Even if, as some believe, that is a later addition to the
book, it exactly expressed Isaiah's sense of just what does mark
the exaltation, power, and transcendence of God—that he is a
blazing power making for righteousness in his world. Hence
Isaiah's bitter exposures of the injustices in a society where the
rich and powerful oppress the weak and the defenseless. This
is most clearly exposed in the brilliantly ironic "Song of the
Vineyard" of 5:1-7, culminating in the bitter puns:

> he expected justice (*mishpat*),
> but saw bloodshed (*mishpah*);
> righteousness (*tsedaqah*),
> but heard a cry (*tseᶜaqah*).

Yet there is still more of the wonder of God glimpsed in
this remarkable vision. For the seraphim who hymn God's
holiness also proclaim, "The whole earth is full of his glory."
The "glory" (Hebrew *kabod*) of God is that of him which
may be visibly apprehended, like the "shekinah" cloud which
comes down and fills the temple in Ezekiel and the "Tent of
Meeting" theology of the Elohistic and Priestly sources of the
Pentateuch. Only here that "glory" is by no means confined to
the temple. It is to be found in every part of the earth. Or, to
put it another way, the vision which reveals the transcendence
of God also stresses his immanence. He is no mere temple
figure, but he breaks out of temple, holy city and even from
among his own people, and involves himself in all creation, in
all human history and all affairs of politics. So the march of
the great power of Assyria is his doing, accomplishing "his
work" (10:12). He can be trusted in international politics so
that it is foolish to trust powers like those of Egypt or Assyria
instead of taking him seriously as a force in human affairs. He
is concerned with the political, social, legal and commercial life
of the nation just as much, indeed, even more, than he is with
the 'religious' affairs of sacrifices and hymns (1:10-17).
No less a God than this is the God who impels his servant
out of the temple into that world to be his messenger and
announce his action. But to what end?

It has to be said that the terms of Isaiah's commission make depressing reading (6:9-13). There is not a glimmer of hope to be found in it, for there can be little doubt that the last line of v. 13 is a later addition. It is missing in the Septuagint; it misses the point of the first part of the verse which is of total annihilation; and the phrase "holy seed" as a description of the people of God is found elsewhere only in late, post-exilic literature (Ezra 9:2). So was Isaiah entirely without hope? Were these words a sad refection by him, or another, at the end of a long ministry, on its apparently total failure? Or are those interpreters right who argue that he was a prophet only of gloom and all the oracles of hope must be later additions to the book? Can we say that the germ of all Isaiah's later message is to be found in this call vision if there is nothing but despair in it?

It is here that one must acknowledge a most important observation of R. Knierim in an article he wrote on this chapter.[1] In a footnote towards the end, he points out that the chapter is not without hope, even apart from the disputed ending of v. 13. For Isaiah himself is cleansed by an act of divine grace (vv. 6-8). Perhaps we can legitimately say that no one who has known anything of the grace of God for him or herself can wholly despair of others. Indeed, it is stressed that Isaiah is there in a representative capacity ("I live among a people of unclean lips"), so that it must be God's purpose to cleanse his people as a whole. Is not the servant of God always a sign of the kingdom as well as a purveyor of words? Do not those who have known God's cleansing grace themselves go amongst the suffering, the sinful, and the despairing as living evidence of the new age, as embodiments of the hope and power of the God who has commissioned and sent them?

It was with the vision of such a God that Isaiah was able to go into all the confusion, the darkness, the fear, and the turmoil of the world of his day and leave a message of hope not only for his own time but for all succeeding days. May it not be that the darkness of our age will be pierced as there go into it those whose eyes have also seen a vision of no less a God than he who appeared to Isaiah as "the King, the LORD of hosts." For us he has appeared above all as the God and Father of our Lord Jesus Christ? As such the God we proclaim and embody can be no smaller than the God of Isaiah's vision.

Notes

[1] R. Knierim, "The Vocation of Isaiah," *Vetus Testamentum* 18 (1968): 47-68.

Chapter Seven
Security Without Might
Isaiah 7:10-20

by Molly T. Marshall-Green
Associate Professor of Theology
The Southern Baptist Theological Seminary
Louisville, Kentucky

Isaiah lived in the rough and tumble world of international politics. God did not allow him to remain in the sanctuary where he had a vision of Yahweh "high and lifted up," but commissioned him to the difficult task of bringing the word of the Lord to an increasingly secular government. Familiar with the corridors of power in Jerusalem, he sought to advise at least four heads of state about God's role and purpose in their national destiny. Diplomacy, "hostile takeovers," treaties, and "foreign aid" oil the machinery of political alignments during his prophetic ministry.

Yahweh called Isaiah to speak the divine word to a beleaguered nation suffering an identity crisis. No longer a mighty power and enduring a strained relationship with its sister kingdom to the north, Judah was tempted to curry favor with a foreign patron in order to protect its own interests, as chapter seven records. Ahaz feared being deposed by an anti-Assyrian coalition, including Ephraim, which threatened to bring an end to the Davidic dynasty upon which so many hopes of the nation rested. Sensing the inherent apostasy in such a decision, Isaiah advised King Ahaz to avoid making political alliances with mighty Assyria in order to obtain a semblance of security. Judah must not forsake her prior commitment, the covenant with Yahweh.

Appealing to Assyria was, in Isaiah's astute judgment, like inviting the camel to stick her nose under the tent; soon she would take over the whole dwelling. Isaiah's prophecy warns Ahaz of the consequences of paying tribute to Assyria in order to ensure Judah's future; his appeal for aid would backfire as the super-power's insatiable appetite would consume the nation's remaining resources. Ahaz would be "shaved with a razor" (7:20); left virtually naked. The image is like a man clothed only in a barrel; everything else had been stripped! Greedy enemies as numerous as flies and bees would overrun the nation, victimizing its people. But if the King of Judah would remain neutral, trusting in God's deliverance, Isaiah assured him that the threat to the house of David would come to naught.

Speaking for Yahweh, the prophet entreated the king to ask for a sign (7:10-11), for God desires that the king seek security in the nation's relationship to their true Sovereign. But Ahaz refuses, feigning piety. "Putting the LORD to the test" was not proper, he demurred. Actually, his words suggest that he does not think Yahweh can be trusted. Isaiah clearly sees through his pretense and denounces him for "wearying" his political colleagues and, more important, he had wearied God also (7:13). Perhaps Ahaz, like some of us, really did not think God could do anything in the political sphere, but was confined to "spiritual" concerns.

Interpreters of the book of Isaiah suggest that the epoch recorded in this narrative is pivotal for the self-understanding of the people of God. The continuity of the Davidic dynasty had been an assurance of God's enduring favor, even when the one inheriting the throne had been a despot. Conflicting interpretations of the dynasty's significance erupted, however, as the nation was partitioned. Where did the true legacy of David reign? Could both northern and southern kingdoms claim the lineage of the paradigmatic king who had brought unity and international respect to Israel?

Questions such as these pressed for answers during the ministry of Isaiah. Ron Clements, a renowned British Baptist Old Testament scholar, says that Isaiah's attitude toward the Davidic dynasty is "more than a little ambiguous."[1] In some instances, the prophet reminded the king of the royal promises ensuring the perpetuity of his throne; on other occasions, Isaiah warned that unfaithful kings should not presume upon God's covenantal mercy when they have abandoned their trust in God.

Interpreters are divided on the question of whether it was the unfaithfulness of Ahaz or the will of God which was reorienting the focus of the Davidic dynasty. John D. W. Watts suggests that in this period "the control of history had been transferred from David's throne to the hand of the Empire."[2] This interpretation suggests that Yahweh is forging a new role for the nation, a servant rather than a ruling vocation. God's primary goal for the nation is for it to bear witness to the nations of the salvation in Yahweh which enables true worship and service. Less a new role than a call to return to their true identity as God's elect, they are to no longer be "a nation like other nations," more concerned about military conquests and regional stature than with serving the living God. The nation could exercise its ministry for God even without the Davidic dynasty to rule over the region, as it once had.

It is not easy for a nation to learn to regard itself in a different way. American identity, for example, has been fueled by certain myths about our generosity, our "rugged individualism," our technological superiority, and our willingness to give everyone a fair chance to accomplish "the American dream" which is usually equated with prosperity. These myths, carefully nurtured across the generations, color our national priorities and policies. At times, however, cataclysmic events can call these ideological assumptions into question, and we realize that as a nation and as individuals we are often more driven by self-interest than largess, and that we are capable of many of the same atrocities of other nations whom we might scorn.

Judah was having a hard time remembering her covenantal vows; not only was the nation being unrealistic about her present context, but she was enamored with her past triumphs. Isaiah was well aware of the harsh experiences that the nation had more recently endured, and he neither wanted the nation's leadership to embark upon foolish political alliances or to seek their security in other than God. Faith in God could be no substitute for judicious political strategy, he reminded the king. Rather, faith would prompt careful listening to the word of God which forewarned him of disastrous national policies.

The dilemma of Ahaz is not foreign to us. But God does not demand that we choose between faith and prudent decision-making, but that we allow our choices to be tempered by an unfailing trust in the faithfulness of God. Some of us need to reflect on our presumption that God will always protect us, no matter what we have chosen. Like the ancient people of God, we cannot easily be spared the consequences of our willful rebellion. Yet God longs to redeem even our wandering when we repent of it.

Even though Ahaz resisted the subdued national role which the prophet envisioned, Isaiah promises, nevertheless, that God will graciously grant a sign of assurance. Here we see the second "sign-child" of the prophet Isaiah. Three children are born to the prophet and his wife, and each of their names carries a message of God's intent for the nation. The first son, Shear-jashub, which means "a remnant will return" accompanied his father as he delivered the message to the king. Now the prophet informs Ahaz that his wife, the young woman (mentioned in verse 14), is pregnant and will bear a child whose name will be Immanuel, which means "God is with us."

Centuries of messianic interpretation have made it hard for us to value properly this historical setting and the child's significance in his own epoch. His name, Immanuel, was meant to serve as an assurance that Judah and her king had nothing to fear from those arrayed against them—unless the king refused to heed the word of God. If he set himself against God, this humble sign of God's presence would remind him of his infidelity, rather than provide comfort. It is characteristic of the humility of God that assurance and divine self-disclosure would come through no more than a helpless child, yet to be born.

Often the birth of Isaiah's second son is confused with the royal birth prophesied in chapter nine. This latter passage refers to a royal accession which promises peace for the people of God. Yet, the two passages have marked similarity in their affirmation that "what appears to be beyond the scope of political possibility has a yet stronger basis of certainty in the divine will."[3]

Isaiah employs the temporal horizon of the expected child in his prophecy about the fate of those who threaten Judah. By the time the child begins eating solid food, "curds and honey," the kings which threaten Ahaz will be incapable of mounting an attack upon him, for their own domestic problems will preoccupy them. If he will but trust Yahweh, he will remain secure without procuring the might of an unreliable neighbor.

The next prediction in the narrative marks a turning point in the passage (7:17). Isaiah pronounces God's judgment upon the nation as a result of the king's unwillingness to allow the promise of God to sustain him and his people. Refusing to believe that the very presence of God (Immanuel) was sufficient, Ahaz could only expect days comparable in devastation to the time when the great kingdom of Solomon was traumatically separated (1 Kgs 12:16-24).

The somber prophecy of 7:18-20 further describes the role surrounding nations will play as God's rod of judgment for the faithless Judah who refused to wait upon Yahweh. How could they even count on divine deliverance when Yahweh no longer had their military superiority to rely upon? Thus, they resisted the vulnerability of trusting in God for their security, and their supposed protectors became the plunderers of their nation.

Most of us find it much easier to hear the voice of God through the personal relationships of our lives, as did Hosea, rather than through the often opaque events of the political scene. When we look to the horizon of history, especially the intense interactions of competing world powers, we realize it is much harder to claim God for one side or the other, and we should be suspicious of those who conscript God for their political agenda. As might be expected, crisp black and white answers blur into the gray of ambiguous choices amidst political intrigue. Yet, God is not absent from the currents of history.

Remarkably, scripture encourages us to persevere through weaving the story of a faithful remnant which continued to hear God's word through these centuries of political unrest and religious confusion. A slender thread of prophets and people continued to believe that God exercises sovereignty in human history even when their own circumstances seemed to betray their faith. Their hope was anchored in the prophet's assurance, "In returning and rest you shall be saved; in quietness and in trust shall be your strength" (Isa 30:15).

Reflecting on the witness of the prophets, Robert Hamerton-Kelly, urges us to take up our responsibility as the remnant of God in our own troubled time. "Who shall be that remnant, if not you and me and all people of faith?"[4] It is the vocation of the remnant of God to remind all humanity that true security is to be found in "Immanuel." This will be a very hard posture to maintain because it stands against our culture's indefatigable attempt to ensure personal security. We think our insurance policies, our savings, our degrees, and ever advancing medical care will secure our futures. But we deceive ourselves. Like Ahaz, we function as if we can do without God as we presume to buy security. Isaiah's warning to the king remains apt, for when we place our trust in other than the abiding presence of God, we can expect those alliances or possessions to become a source of judgment to us.

The prophet promised the king that there would be a concrete sign that "God is with us." Humans are so put together that we need such reminders of the presence of God. Perhaps in our day, the best sign of God's presence is a people committed to God's way in their worship and service. Communities of faith do not find their strength through their material resources, but through their mutual trust in God's faithfulness. Their shared hope in the promise of God provides a "hospitable space" (Henri Nouwen's term) which makes welcome others seeking a safe place.

When we reflect on "security without might," we think not only about our own weakness, but we remember that God comes to us not as the expected heir of David's throne, but in the humility of a peasant's poverty and a criminal's scandalous death. We may surely trust that God is "mighty to save," but the means may surprise even those faithful to the remnant's task. What will not surprise us is that our security is always because God is with us.

Notes

[1] R. E. Clements, *Isaiah 1-29*, The New Century Bible Commentary (Grand Rapids: Eerdmans Publishing, 1980), p. 108.

[2] John D. W. Watts, *Isaiah 1-33*, Word Biblical Commentary (Waco: Word Books, 1985), p. lvi.

[3] Clements, p. 109.

[4] Robert G. Hamerton-Kelly, *The Divine Passion: Reflections on the Prophets* (Nashville: The Upper Room, 1988), p. 47.

Chapter Eight
A Preview of Coming Attractions
Isaiah 9:1-7

by James M. Pitts
Chaplain, Furman University
Greenville, South Carolina

Imagine living in a land where it is always winter and never Christmas. Life would be cold and flat, colorless and dull. Mortal existence would be a limited landscape, outlined in blue and washed with monochromes of gray. No parties or presents, no festive meals filled with remembrance or lively conversations underscoring shared anticipation.

In a land where it is always winter and never Christmas, every day is the same. Routine replaces celebrations. Mere survival and the meeting of basic needs take precedence over the luxury and leisure of a holiday. Life is without accent. Unadorned, the trees are without ornaments and lights. There is no candle in the window signaling welcome to friends in the dark.

Residing in a land where it is always winter and never Christmas describes the experience of many. Some are preoccupied with the prospect or reality of family members or friends in the military being deployed to the Persian Gulf. Others are maintaining a bedside vigil with children who are sick or with parents who are terminally ill. Some are painfully aware of empty chairs at holiday tables, which underscore their loss and loneliness.

In their year end and beginning assessments, television

commentators and their learned guests announce difficult times are not only ahead, but here. The economy is troubled. The hushed "R" word of recession, once denied, is now spoken freely. Business is experiencing "D.T.'s" or a down turn. "Nothing is wrong with America," one cynic quipped, "that a depression or World War III won't cure."

Political consensus is increasingly difficult to achieve. Nationally, single issue debates fragment and polarize. Internationally, new alliances are being forged with old enemies, and relationships are being tested by those we presumed to be enduring friends.

From our limited perspective, it seems the entire world is uneasy. The whole human family appears to be living on stand by. The shift from the old to the new, from yesteryear to the world tomorrow, has potential for societal self-destruction or creative reintegration. Watching and waiting, we are looking for a sign or signal that will give us a future and a hope, a sense of courage and confidence.

We long for the innocence of childhood, when we could be cradled in our parent's arms, hugged and lovingly reassured that everything is going to be O.K. Wouldn't it be nice to hear that we are going to be safe and secure, and sheltered from all harm? Being older and wiser, and certainly more cynical, we push aside such thinking as childish regression.

Some seven hundred years before the birth of the Christ child, the land of Judah and the city of Jerusalem were residing in the shadows. The good old days were gone. The golden age of King David was a only an idyllic memory.

The Northern Kingdom had fallen and was annexed to the expanding Assyrian Empire (2 Kgs 17). The Southern Kingdom's days of independence were numbered. Contributions were being made from their treasury to Assyria but to no avail (2 Chr 28:21). The people were discouraged and depressed. There was much confusion and great disarray. Hope was in short supply.

The situation addressed by the prophet Isaiah has contemporary relevance. Both then and now, the Middle East is a scene of economic and political power struggles, complicated by religious conflict. Then and now, there and here, we see a harvest of shame. We gather the bitter fruits of self-centered pride, greed, indifference to human need, and disregard for the righteous will of a universal God.

Like Isaiah's contemporaries, we, too, walk in darkness and in the shadow of death. They were threatened with exile. Today, Arab residents are subject to deportation from Jerusalem and its environs. Here in America, environmentalists warn that we are poisoning our wells, exploiting our land, and running the risk of becoming exiles from the earth itself. Like those people of old, we too need light to illuminate our darkness and leadership to show us the way to a new and better day.

As a discerning witness of God at work in our world, Isaiah declares the will and word of God. With moral certainty and spiritual understanding, he analyses a critical situation, announces judgment, and offers hope. I invite you to listen to God's word for that time and reflect upon its relevance for our here and now.

In Isaiah 9:1-7 the prophet has two main hopes. First, he longs for the deliverance of Judah from foreign invasion, and second, he anticipates the establishment of justice and good government among the people of the land.

Projecting himself into the future, the prophet imagines the ideal age as already realized. Darkness has been transformed into light. The people, freed from oppression and war, are filled with joy. They have been provided a king who embodies what kingship should have been, but had failed to be. Note there is no mention of material prosperity, expanded territory, or a mighty army.

These hymn-like phrases move from doom to promise. They represent a perfect Davidic monarchy and may have been originally used to celebrate the ascension of King Hezekiah. They describe the best qualities of Israel's heroes (Ezek 37:25).

This is an ideal king, strong and authentic, exhibiting parental love and care, bringing peace to the land. Throughout Israel's history, continually on the horizon of religious expectation, was this exalted and mysterious person. There was the hope for an anointed one, a messiah.

Isaiah's announcement underscores the popular longing for a glorious son of David. This was especially acute when the throne was occupied by an unworthy individual, such as King Ahaz. He was seen as a fool and a traitor. With the nation threatened with complete devastation, the people feeling exhausted, only something fresh and straight from God could help revive their spirit.

This "Prince of Four Names" has an earthly and civil function: "Wonderful Counselor"—one who gives sound advice; "Mighty God"—one who has the strength of God in him as he administers justice; "Everlasting Father"—one who expresses continuing parental love and care as the one who heads the nation; "Prince of Peace"—a king who brings peace and prosperity.

Combining political and spiritual ideals, this king is righteous, just, compassionate and mighty in defense of the weak. Here in the prophetic imagination, there is a spiritual aspiration which transcends earthly experience. The prophet speaks of a king and a kingdom.

We find in Isaiah a varying emphasis between a personal messiah and a messianic kingdom; a religious community and a political state; a new order in human relationships which is extended to the whole realm of nature.

Isaiah had a confident belief that God would fulfill his holy purpose for Judah and for the world. A new day was dawning. The people were living between memory and hope. It was time to move from the dirge of doom to the song of promise.

Israel reached the pinnacle of its glory under the reign of David, before Solomon's tyranny divided the Kingdom. They longed for a restoration of vanished grandeur. Some patriotic Jews dreamed of a new Israel under some descendant of David. The expected, ideal king, would be the anointed one, a messiah. In God's good time and through his initiative, a new golden age would come.

Isaiah's messianic king (9:1-6 and 11:1-9) stands in sharp contrast to the suffering servant, which the book of Isaiah presents in its later chapters. Yet the four names in chapter 9 have the same basic meaning as those presented in Isaiah 11.

> The Spirit of the Lord shall rest on him,
> the spirit of wisdom and understanding,

the spirit of counsel and might,
the spirit of knowledge and fear of the LORD (11:2).

This ruler will judge, not by appearance, but according to truth and justice. He will thwart the wicked, uphold the poor and lowly. Righteousness and faithfulness will be the source of his strength.

This new order will not be founded on racial pride, hatred, or armaments. There will be harmony in creation and a reverence for life, where God's purpose will embrace and undergird the whole creation of nature and humankind.

For the Christian, a redeemer appeared that both fulfilled and exceeded Isaiah's dream. In his book, *Isaiah Speaks*, Paul Schilling writes,

> Clearly these prophecies did not specifically predict the coming of Jesus of Nazareth. However, in the deepest sense they were fulfilled in him. As the generations passed, no leader appeared who even approximated Isaiah's picture of the Anointed One. But after the last king of Judah had died in exile in Babylon, the hope persisted that God would yet send a Davidic king to lead his people into a new age. Enriched and deepened by Second Isaiah, that hope was cherished in the long baffling centuries of struggle and subjection, until finally a Redeemer appeared who exceeded Isaiah's fondest dreams. "When the time had fully come, God sent forth his son" (Gal 4:4). The expectations long treasured by the prophets prepared the way for Jesus, truly the anointed one. Isaiah had spoken better than he knew. The ideal earthly king had never come, but the Christ who has come displays a truer royalty. The perfect earthy state remains a dream, but God has founded in Jesus Christ a spiritual community of love and righteousness, which makes all things new.[1]

"For unto us a child is born," reminds Christians of the joyous announcement of Advent. Central for the believing community is the Christ child, the baby born in Bethlehem. Yet such retroactive clarity is evident only by Christian hindsight. In In Herb Gardner's play, "I'm Not Rappaport" we see two old men sitting on a bench in New York's Central Park. They are enraged by society's neglect and rejection of the elderly. One yells out to a young pedestrian who looks aside, turning his gaze away from the old men on the bench, as he walks past.

The elderly gentlemen challenges him not to look away, but to look them in the eye. "Don't ignore us or act like we don't exist." "After all," the old guy announces, "we are a preview of a coming attraction. Some day you will be assigned to a bench and will look as old, wrinkled, and worn as we are" (author's paraphrase).

Friends, if we live, we are going to age. But the promise of life is more than simply growing old. There is the assurance of life beyond the shadows. This is not achieved by a nostalgic yearning for the past, or a rejecting denial of the present. It comes with a hopeful anticipation of the future. A preview of coming attractions is revealed in the one who represents the yearnings of countless generations. This preview for each and all of us is personified for the believer in Jesus.

Jesus is our preview of coming attractions. Through him we have a sure sign and divine signal of God's participation in history, and the promise of redemption and resurrection. This is not a result of human striving, but of God's initiation and achievement. As Isaiah states, "The zeal of the LORD of Hosts will do this" (11:7).

The new day, the messianic kingdom, is dependent on divine action. The faithful remnant waits with humility, trustful of God's response.

Our hope and trust in God transcend the immediate. It began a long time ago with the birth of baby, it centered on a cross, and was unclouded before an empty tomb. In worship, we affirm our hope and trust today, counting on Christ to carry us through our tomorrows and into eternity with him.

Reinhold Niebuhr reminds us:

> Nothing that is worth doing can be achieved in a lifetime; therefore we must be saved by hope.
> Nothing which is true and beautiful or good makes complete sense in any immediate context of history; therefore we must be saved by faith.
> Nothing we do, however, virtuous, can be accomplished alone. Therefore, we are saved by love.[2]

Notes

[1] S. Paul Schilling, *Isaiah Speaks* (New York: Women's Division of Christian Service, Board of Missions of the Methodist Church, 1958), p. 73.

[2] Reinhold Niebuhr, *The Irony of American History* (New York: Charles

Chapter Nine

The Promise of Paradise Regained

Isaiah 11:1-9

by Jon M. Stubblefield

Pastor, First Baptist Church
Shreveport, Louisiana

As twentieth century Christians who ponder this text, we point to the ultimate fulfillment of all prophetic hopes in the coming of Jesus Christ. The messianic hope introduced in Isaiah 7:10-17 and developed in 9:2-7 finds further expression in 11:1-9.[1]

Originally this text may have been used in the celebration of the accession of a Judean king. Its structure consists of three strophes or stanzas: the announcement of the ideal king and his spiritual qualities (11:1-3a); the characteristics of his reign (11:3b-5); and the resulting peace and harmony his rule will bring (11:6-9). From Isaiah's perspective the vision focused not on some shadowy figure in the distant future but on a king who would reign as part of the Davidic dynasty. The enthronement of each new ruler invited the hope that he would usher in the golden age. With the exile, however, the hope shifted to the promise of the messiah.[2]

The message of Isaiah 11:1-9 has filtered down to us through 2700 years of interpretation. For our purpose we will consider three abiding truths that flow out of the text. They relate to God's power, God's presence, and God's purpose in the realization of paradise regained.

God's power brings life out of death and transforms something small and insignificant into that which is great and significant. The closing verses of Isaiah 10 and the beginning of chapter 11 stand in sharp juxtaposition. The prophet pronounced the downfall of Assyria, depicted as a mighty forest being cut down (10:33-34). The Lord, the Master Forester, will wield the ax of his judgment to level the empire, leaving behind rotting stumps on the mountainside. By way of contrast, from the "stump of Jesse" a "shoot" will spring forth and "a branch shall grow out of his roots" (11:1).

Isaiah prophesied when Ahaz was on the throne. A succession of kings followed from Hezekiah to Zedekiah, and with them the gradual decline and deterioration of the kingdom. With the coronation of each new ruler, the people exclaimed with anticipation, "Perhaps this is Messiah, the Promised One." But each new hope was dashed to the ground. Finally in 587 B.C. the Babylonian army plundered Jerusalem and pillaged the king's palace. The throne of David assumed the appearance of a lifeless stump.

Would the vision of Isaiah ever be realized? How could the line of David be reborn from a dead stump? Centuries came and went. Domination by the Babylonians gave way to the Persians, then to the Greeks, and ultimately to the Romans. At last a new day dawned, and a light broke through the darkness. "But when the fullness of time had come" (Gal 4:4), a healthy "shoot" sprouted from the "stump of Jesse" and a "branch" (*netser*) grew out of its roots. Perhaps Matthew had the word *netser* in mind when he recalled "what was spoken by the prophets" that the messiah would be called a "Nazorean" (Matt 2:23).[3] Certainly the writer of Revelation drew upon Isaiah's vision with the reference to Jesus Christ as the "Root of David" (Rev 5:5).[4]

A peasant couple lived in a forgotten village in the vast Roman Empire. What contribution could they make to the eternal plan of God? Yet history recounts their story. Joseph and Mary made the long trip from Nazareth in Galilee to the unlikely spot called Bethlehem. While there Mary "gave birth to her first-born son and wrapped him in bands of cloth, and laid him in a manger" (Luke 2:7). God kept faith with his promise. Out of the "stump of Jesse" came tender new life.

God's power also was at work a thousand years earlier. Commanded by God Samuel went to Bethlehem to anoint a new king in the place of disobedient Saul. Seven sons of the shepherd Jesse paraded before the prophet, but each in turn was rejected as God's designated heir to the throne. At last the youngest son, David, was called in from the field. Surely he was not a likely candidate for such an important task! But when Samuel saw David God told him, "Rise and anoint him; for this is the one" (1 Sam 16:1-13). Little is much when God is in it.

This same David carried an ordinary shepherd's sling. Not worth much some would say. God used it, however, to defeat proud Goliath, the defiant Philistine. A boy's lunch consisted of five loaves and two fish. Enough to feed a hungry crowd? Placed in the hands of God it was more than enough!

The mustard seed was known as "the smallest of all the seeds on earth" (Mark 4:31). Nevertheless, when planted it produced a mature shrub that put forth branches capable of providing nests and shade for the birds. Jesus employed the mustard seed as an illustration to depict the dramatic growth of the kingdom of God. Who could have predicted that a small band of Jesus' followers, fishermen, tax collectors, and the like, would be able to turn the world upside down with the Gospel?

We may think our lives are as useless as a dead old stump, that nothing good can ever come from them. However, God can take what we offer him, bless it, and use it to help accomplish his redemptive purpose in the world. God's power brings life out of death and transforms something useless into that which is useful.

God's presence though his Spirit endows his servants to perform their tasks. The announcement of the appearance of the ideal king is followed by his equipment for service. "The Spirit of the LORD shall rest upon him" (11:2a). Both Saul and David had been endued with God's Spirit (1 Sam. 10:10, 16:13), but later an "evil spirit" came over Saul (1 Sam 18:10), and David, following his sin, prayed "do not take your holy spirit from me" (Ps 51:11). John N. Oswalt writes, the Davidic kings Isaiah knew "had come to manifest a spirit which had little of God in it."[5] Their spiritual bankruptcy eventually led the prophet to conclude that the palace would be "forsaken" until God's Spirit visited his people (Isa 32:14-15).

According to Isaiah, in the messianic age God's Spirit will "rest" upon his servant, that is, abide in a permanent way. His equipment will include three pairs of gifts (11:2b). The first two focus on his wisdom; the second pair, his administrative qualities; and the third pair, his piety or reverence.

God's anointed will be the perfect ruler (11:3-5). He will not judge by outward appearances but will champion the causes of the oppressed and deal severely with the wicked. "Righteousness" and "faithfulness" will be his clothing. Righteousness is the ability to do the right thing in all circumstances; and faithfulness denotes integrity, consistency and complete dependability.[6]

The portrait of this ideal king found human expression in Jesus of Nazareth. The Holy Spirit came upon human flesh, and from the womb of Mary a baby was born in Bethlehem. At his baptism the Holy Spirit descended on Jesus like a dove. A voice from heaven sounded, "This is my Son, the beloved" (Matt 3:17). This statement echoes Psalm 2:7, part of a coronation hymn used at the crowning of a king. God's king was being crowned to rule over his people. The voice also acknowledged, "with whom I am well pleased." This expression comes from Isaiah 42:1 and described the Suffering Servant in whom the Lord delights. Jesus was hailed as both King and Servant (Mark 1:9-11).

In the synagogue at Nazareth Jesus announced that the Spirit of the Lord was upon him (Luke 4:18-19). Recalling the words of Isaiah (61:1-2; 58:6), he defined his ministry in terms of preaching good news to the poor, proclaiming release to the captives, restoring sight to the blind, setting at liberty the oppressed and proclaiming "the year of the Lord's favor."

Clearly the Spirit rested on Jesus in a permanent way, but God's abiding presence also belonged to Jesus' followers. On the day of his resurrection Jesus appeared to his disciples. After he breathed on them, he commanded, "Receive the Holy Spirit" (John 20:22). The Spirit would equip them for service as well.

As believers who have part in the continuing incarnation, we can appropriate the power of the Holy Spirit. The Holy Spirit takes up permanent residence at the moment of conversion. When the wind of God's Spirit blows across our lives, we experience a new birth (John 3:1-8). The Holy Spirit guides us in all truth (John 16:13) and enables us to bear fruit (Gal 5:22-23). Although we may grieve the Spirit (Eph 4:30) and quench the Spirit's work (1 Thess 5:19), the Holy Spirit continually intercedes for us (Rom 8:26-27). When we allow God's Spirit to equip and empower us for service, we begin to comprehend, albeit it in a limited way, the meaning of the messianic age.

God's purpose is the redemption and restoration of all creation. Isaiah's vision of the messianic age concludes with a poetic picture of paradise regained (11:6-9). Wild and domestic animals will dwell together in perfect harmony. Wolf and lamb, leopard and kid, cow and bear will cease to be mortal enemies. Imagine a carnivorous lion eating straw like an ox! (11:7). Moreover, little children will not be afraid of deadly snakes. No creature will be allowed to injure or destroy any other creature. Both the social order and nature will be transformed so that "the earth will be full of the knowledge of the LORD as the waters cover the sea" (11:9b). The knowledge described is personal, not intellectual or theoretical.

The people of Isaiah's time did not see the fulfillment of his prophecy. Neither has it come to pass in our day. To be sure, the messianic age dawned with the incarnation, and with confidence we can affirm that some day paradise will be regained.

The messianic age was inaugurated with Jesus' birth. He was born in a manger, presumably surrounded by animals. An angel accompanied by "a multitude of the heavenly host" sang praises to God (Luke 2:13). Humble shepherds and regal wise men, representing human diversity, paid homage to the newborn king. A bright star hovered "over the place where the child was" (Matt 2:9). Celestial life, animal life, human life, and nature converged to celebrate Jesus' birth. Did the Gospel writers intend to symbolize that all creation ultimately will acknowledge Jesus as Messiah and Lord?

The messianic age continued in the ministry of Jesus.

Wild beasts were present with him during his temptation experience in the wilderness (Mark 1:13). This detail perhaps identified Jesus as the Second Adam who had come to recreate Eden.[7] His miracles demonstrated God's power at work in the new age. As the strong Son of God he was able to bind Satan (Mark 3:23-27). He was regarded also as Lord of all. He was Lord over nature, over the mind, over the body, and even over death (Mark 4:35-5:34). His coming meant redemption and promised the restoration of all creation.

The messianic age becomes personalized in individual experience. The same Jesus who put the Gergasene demoniac in his right mind can tame the wild beasts in us. He makes the wolf and the lamb lie down together. He offers peace and purpose to troubled hearts.

A young man knocked at my study door. He wanted to talk, so I listened. Without hesitation he blurted out a sordid story. Alcohol and drugs, association with the wrong crowd, and immoral conduct had almost ruined his life. He wanted to know the way back to God. I told him about God's love and how Jesus Christ died for him. As we prayed he invited Christ into his life. The messianic age dawned in his experience.

The messianic age will culminate with the redemption and restoration of all creation. Every knee will bow and every tongue will confess Jesus Christ as Lord (Phil 2:10-11). At present, however, "we do not yet see everything in subjection" (Heb 2:8).

Paul viewed creation as "groaning in labor pains" (Rom 8:22). Along with human beings the natural world has suffered the devastating effects of sin. The evidence is not hard to find. It is recounted daily in newspapers and on nightly network news broadcasts. Reports of overpopulation and starvation, the depletion of natural resources, toxic waste, acid rain, air and water pollution and global warming trends remind us that Isaiah's vision is far from being realized. Instead of working with God for the restoration of creation, we are bent on the destruction of our planet. As Christians we have an ethical responsibility to take an active role in the preservation of our environment and oppose actions of selfishness and greed that hasten its demise.

We still await the day when everything hurtful and destructive will be subdued by Christ.

"For the earth will be full of the knowledge of the LORD as the waters cover the sea" (11:9). Then we will understand fully, even as we have been fully understood (1 Cor 13:12b).

Notes

[1] These companion passages often serve as the basis for Christmas sermons. For a helpful discussion on how to approach selected messianic texts in Isaiah (including chapter 11), see Holland Jones, "How I Would Use Messianic Prophecy in Advent," *Currents in Theology and Mission* 9 (December, 1982): 354-359.

[2] G. G. D. Kilpatrick, "The Book of Isaiah" (Exposition), *The Interpreter's Bible*, vol. 5 (Nashville: Abingdon Press, 1956), pp. 247-248.

[3] On the possible connection between *netser* and "Nazarene," see Raymond E. Brown, *The Birth of the Messiah* (Garden City, New York: Image Books, 1979), pp. 211-213, 219. "The strongest positive indication lies in the fact that the branch which will blossom from the root of Jesse (Isa. 11:1) is the child Emmanuel whose forthcoming birth had been announced in Isa. 7:14. Since Matthew applied the latter passage to Jesus in 1:22-23, it is not unlikely that he was still thinking in terms of the Isaian description of the Davidic royal child" (p. 212).

[4] Jesus also is referred to as "the root and the offspring of David" (Rev. 22:16).

[5] John N. Oswalt, *The Book of Isaiah: Chapters 1-39*, The New International Commentary on the Old Testament (Grand Rapids: Eerdmans Publishing, 1986), p. 279.

[6] Ibid., p. 282.

[7] Different interpretations have been advanced regarding the presence of wild beasts. Some scholars hold that they signified the loneliness of the location or symbolized the presence of evil. See Ernest Best, *The Temptation and the Passion: The Markan Soteriology*, Society for New Testament Studies Monograph Series 2 (Cambridge: University Press, 1965), pp. 7-9.

Chapter Ten
Worth Waiting For
Isaiah 25:1-9

by Allen Walworth
Pastor, First Baptist Church
Huntsville, Alabama

Florence Martus was just a young girl in 1888. But Savannah, Georgia was already a grown up seaport, with maritime commerce connecting the city to distant and exotic ports of call around the world. In such a city, lovers like Florence and her sailor were common. They barely knew each other when he asked her to marry him. His shore leave gave them time to fall in love, and time for her to say "yes" to his proposal, but not enough time to get married before his ship left Savannah harbor. Time can be cruel. He promised he would come back for her. She promised she would wait for him. And with fresh promises and high hope, the lovers were parted by the tides and oceans.

And wait she did. But for Florence Martus, waiting was not a passive activity. From her house by the entrance to the harbor she greeted each ship which docked in Savannah port by waving a cloth by day, and a lantern by night. When her sailor returned for her, she wanted to be the first person to welcome him home. She wanted to wait for him with a face. Between ships she would anesthetize her longing with preparations for a grand wedding feast to which everyone would be invited. But he didn't come. For fifty years Florence Martus greeted sailors from around the world to Savannah, all in the hope of greeting the promised one for whom she waited. But her ship didn't come in. The marriage never happened. Time won. She became known as "the waving girl" to the sailors. And upon her death in 1938 a bronze likeness of her familiar pose was placed at the entrance to Savannah harbor to welcome the ships. Perhaps to honor her for waiting so faithfully and tragically. Perhaps because the sailors entering Savannah harbor, like the rest of us, needed someone to wait for them. It is the light which guides us all home.

But it's hard work—waiting. And for most of us, a tiresome task indeed. From doctors offices to airport terminals to red lights, our litany of protest against waiting rises. To wait seems an affront to our sense of importance, to our urgency of schedule. It is simply a waste of our most precious commodity—time. Those who market gadgets for the consumer have certainly heard the litany. Microwave ovens now bake the potato in four minutes, yet we still pat our foot anxiously as we watch the seconds tick off the oven timer. Cassette and video tape high-speed rewinders now do the job in five seconds that used to take all of thirty seconds before. We have fallen to the tyranny of the instant—demanding instant coffee, instant dinner rolls, and instant developed film. We want minute rice and "one minute management." We buy sod for lawns rather than plant and nurture the grass from seed. Let's face it, for the busy and the impatient, the new currency is time.[1] And the greatest waste of this currency is waiting. So, give us convenience stores without check-out lines, overnight delivery and fax machines without waiting for the mail. We would rather pay more cash than pay more time. It's not so much that we have something else more pressing to do, rather we have something we do not want to do—wait. It's hard work, and frustrating, this business of waiting.

But not all waiting is frustrating, it is also one of our chief forms of fun. There is an inherent pleasure in waiting, a delayed gratification which is intensified by the very waiting which we so often avoid. Remember the Heinz catsup commercial with its advertised rich and thick (and *slow*) catsup which creeps from the bottle to the hot dog to the tune of "anticipation"? And does not the *smell* of the meal cooking add as much pleasure to the feast as the *taste*? Note the rebellion of the senses when a catered meal instantly served robs one of the delicacy of savored aromas from the kitchen or grill. And what child has not learned to eat frosted cake by eating the cake first and saving the sweet icing for last? We enhance life's pleasure by delay—by waiting. In the same way, the preparation and anticipation for a family vacation may be more enjoyable than the actual trip itself. Even Christmas Day is often anticlimactic compared to the joy of anticipating and planning it. And the fun of waiting extends to cinematic and literary narratives as well. The plot is thickened (like good catsup), and our attention and enjoyment is sustained, by suspending the resolution of the mystery or the consummation of the romance or the completion of the quest until the end. Admit it, we enjoy the waiting sometimes; the dissonant chord resolved only in the last measure of the musical score, the birthday present opened with deliberate and agonizing slowness, the dessert saved for last after the meal. If our desires are worth waiting for, the waiting can be half the fun.

This is Isaiah's point to his hearers weary of waiting for the redemption of God and the ushering of the Kingdom. Like a parent driving the family car on vacation, God listens to our laments as children captive in the back seat. "Aren't we there *yet?* How much longer?" God's children, then and now, are involved in a journey of faith without firm knowledge of the journey's course, and only a vague image of its destination. Aren't we there yet? How much longer must we wait on God? Where is God—and where is God's Kingdom of justice and peace? From what we can see looking out on life's journey from the back seat windows, we only know we're not there yet.

And so God has a word of encouragement. The text re-sings the song of hope that began the journey in the first place:

> O LORD, you are my God . . .
> for you have done wonderful things,
> plans formed of old, faithful and sure (25:1)

which means for the weary traveller, "trust the God who brought you this far." When our hopes and prayers go un-answered, when injustice and ruthlessness run rampant, God is not absent—nor absent-minded. God just winds God's own clock. God sets God's own schedule. And the God who planned today yesterday, Isaiah says, will bring about today's tomorrow.[2] And in the meantime, when we are tempted to rush to lesser but more immediate security, he reminds us:

> For you have made the city a heap . . .
>   it will never be rebuilt.
> For you have been a refuge to the poor,
>   a refuge to the needy in their distress,
> A shelter from the rainstorm and
>   a shade from the heat.
> When the blast of the ruthless was
>   like a winter rainstorm,
>   the noise of aliens like heat in a dry place,
>   you subdued the head with the shade of the clouds;
>   the song of the ruthless was stilled (25:2-5).

Here is the song of those who trust God against all odds, in the face of all the contrary evidence. It is the ballad of the poor who have no other options and no other advocates but to trust God. And we are bid to sing the song with them, to resist the imitation music of the sirens which lures us to ground our hope against the rocks of military alliances and economic power.

But when? When will God bring about this hope? How can we trust when life seems untrustworthy? How can we remain sheep in a world dominated by wolves? How can we believe in the dawn when the night is so dark? Isaiah answers with one word—wait. It is the chorus of many of Isaiah's prophetic stanzas:

> I will wait for the LORD, who is hiding his face from the house of Jacob, and I will hope in him (8:17).

> Therefore the LORD waits to be gracious to you;
> therefore he will rise up to show mercy to you.
> For the LORD is a God of justice;
> blessed are all those who wait for him (30:18).

> But those who wait for the LORD shall renew their strength,
> they shall mount up with wings like eagles,
> they shall run and not be weary,
> they shall walk and not faint (40:31).

Those who wait for me shall not be put to shame (49:23) .

In the path of your judgments, O LORD, we wait for you;
your name and your renown are the soul's desire (26:8).

O LORD, be gracious to us; we wait for you.
Be our arm every morning, our salvation in the time of trouble
(33:2).

From ages past no one has heard, no ear has perceived,
no eye has seen any God besides you,
who works for those who wait for him (64:4).

Waiting. Not a waste of time, but a passive power which trusts
the faithfulness of an active God. It is only the power of
waiting which can transform night into day, winter into spring,
child into adult. Yes, there are some things in life we may *work*
for. But there are also some treasures in life one must *wait* for.
We get the chicken by hatching the egg, not by smashing it.
The seed grows by being left alone in the soil, not by digging
it up each day for status checks. And the banquet of God when
"all peoples" shall feast at God's table—the destination of the
human journey—is being prepared even now in the kitchen of
God's grace and patience.[3] We catch only a faint taste of the
feast in an occasional hors d'oeuvre of peace or morsel of
human kindness, and our palate is quickened.[4] But it will be
worth the wait, says Isaiah. And along with the tantalizing
taste and aroma of the banquet, Isaiah cracks the door of hope
that we might also overhear the song of those who celebrate
the communion with God and each other around the table.
Listen to them:

Lo, this is our God; we have waited for him,
    so that he might save us.
This is the LORD for whom we have waited;
    let us be glad and rejoice in his salvation (25:9).

It is the song of those who waited. It is the song of the
redeemed. And there, singing with the best of them, is Florence
Martus, her cheeks freshly wiped of their tears by the hands of

a tender God who has been waiting all this time for all of us to come home for dinner.

So what are we waiting for?

Notes

[1] See the perceptive discussion of this matter in George Barna, *The Frog in the Kettle: What Christians Need to Know About Life in the Year 2000* (Ventura, California: Regal Books, 1990), p. 39.

[2] John Oswalt, *The Book of Isaiah: Chapters 1-39*, The New International Commentary on the Old Testament (Grand Rapids: Eerdmans Publishing, 1986), pp. 460-461.

[3] For discussion of the divine banquet image in ancient Near Eastern mythology, see John D. W. Watts, *Isaiah 1-33*, Word Biblical Commentary (Waco: Word Books, 1985), pp. 330-333.

[4] The description of the feast in vv. 6-8 may not be too appetizing for contemporary readers. "A feast of things" indicates the prized status of fatty portions of meat, which were considered the best part (see Pss 36:8; 63:5) and were usually reserved for sacrifices to God (Lev 3:3; 4:8-9). Here God gives back the portions offered in worship by serving them at the banquet of the faithful. "The feast of lees" refers to wine which is strengthened by leaving the dregs in the wine longer than the normal fermenting process. A feast of strong wine and high cholesterol content fats may not make all contemporary readers salivate, but for Isaiah's hearers, these are the images of the very best of God's plenty.

Chapter Eleven
The Peace of God
Isaiah 26:1-4

by *Charles B. Bugg*
Carl E. Bates
Professor of Christian Preaching
The Southern Baptist Theological Seminary
Louisville, Kentucky

At times the Bible is amazingly simple. "Thou wilt keep him in perfect peace whose mind is stayed on Thee." That is the way the more well-known King James Version renders verse 4. Said so simply. To the nation of Israel then; to the people of God now—they are simple words, "Thou wilt keep him in perfect peace whose mind is stayed on Thee."

Those of us who are ministers need to remember the power of saying something simply. Maurice Boyd, pastor of the Fifth Avenue Presbyterian Church in New York City, reminds us how God spoke to Noah, "Noah, build yourself an ark because it's going to rain." Could you imagine how that might come out in our wordy world? "Noah," God might have said, "we have to dialogue! There is a flood situation. The scenario weather-wise, as of right now, is a one hundred percent chance of precipitation. And it's going to impact real soon in terms of water."[1] Too much! "Noah, build yourself an ark because it's going to rain." That says what needs to be said.

"Thou wilt keep him in perfect peace . . . " the writer says, and it is simple. But, at the same time, it is powerfully profound. What is it that the nation of Israel needed more than anything else in the prophet's time? Shalom! Peace! That sense of balance and well-being even when things around us are changing, chaotic, and confusing. And what is it that we need in our time more than anything else? That same sense of stability and strength.

We search for it in a variety of ways. Nations look for peace in a "balance of power." But like the school-yard see-saw, just about the time that we get it right, somebody else decides to get on, and the balance is lost. And so nations continue to spend billion of dollars trying to keep a precarious peace.

As individuals we also look for peace. Is there a pill, a book by Shirley MacLaine, or a guru on the Himalayan mountainside that can give us something to satisfy? The search in our day is for peace. It is not funny. We all are desperately hungry for something that will feed our spirits. I need it. You need it. We all need it. How do we conquer inner space, and the prophets of peace can be found on the bookshelves of the Mall bookstore, hawking their solutions to unwary passengers at the airport, and even on television promising all that we need for life if we call their "900" number.

The search is on for peace. But when we read these words of Isaiah, we realize that the search has always been on. For the people of God in the prophet's day, the question was "How do we find a constant in a world of change?" "Where can we find firm footing when the sands shift?" Israel knew what change was. Their history was one of change. Peace and wars, security and exile, temples and tents. Israel knew about the up's and down's and in's and out's of life. Somehow, the people needed to find a focus when so much of life seemed out of focus. "Thou wilt keep him in perfect peace whose mind is stayed on Thee," the prophet said.

That promise has both human and a divine side. From our side the word is trust. Twice Isaiah uses that word in these four verses. The word is trust.

You may remember the words of the Queen to Alice in *Through the Looking Glass*. The Queen was upset with young Alice because she would not believe some outrageous claim the Queen had made about her age. Finally, in disgust the Queen chided Alice, "Why sometimes I've believed as many as six impossible things before breakfast."

What do we think of when we think of faith? Intellectual

assent? Believing the unbelievable? When the Bible speaks of faith, it is usually talking about a commitment of life. "Trust," Isaiah pleaded. Realize that you cannot do life by yourself; realize your dependence; then trust God with your life. I look at a chair and say I believe that will hold me. That's intellectual assent. I sit in the chair. That's trust. I sit by the side of the pool with my feet dangling in the water and think that this water will hold me up. That's intellectual assent. I get in and do the back float. That's trust. I affirm marriage as an institution. That's intellectual assent. One day I stand in the front of a church and say, "I do." That's trust.

Trust has a risky element to it. I don't stand at arm's length from God and say, "I believe." I put my life in God's hands and say, "I do." From our side the word is trust.

From God's side the word is "keep." "Thou wilt keep Him in perfect peace . . . ." Sometimes in the preaching classes that I teach I will encourage the students to listen to the lyrics of some country music songs. "I've been ruthless since Ruth walked out on me," one song says, and it reminds us how close tears and laughter are to each other. The words are funny, but remember a time when somebody rejected you. The one thing that you were not doing was laughing.

Or what about this less than immortal line, "You're the reason our kids are ugly, little darlin'." Talk about handling anger. What happened to the young couple at the front of the church who pledged to love each other "for better and for worse." Now, a few children later, it's "You're the reason our kids are ugly, little darlin'."

Things have a way of changing, and dreams sometimes get shattered. The best hopes for life, for marriage, for children, for career, for whatever...most all of us know what it is to deal with brokenness. Change is the name of the game of life, and the question is, "Where do we turn?"

In February, 1983, when our ten-year old, David, was diagnosed with a critical illness, the doctors told our family, "We have to take it one day at a time." That has been over eight years ago of days and nights, times when he has done well and times when we have watched David suffer. I never expected this kind of illness to strike our family, but then none of us ever does, do we? Life changes. The firm footing is suddenly shifting sand. "Where do we turn?"

"To God," Isaiah answers. "Thou wilt keep him in perfect peace whose mind is stayed on Thee." That is the promise. It is simple. Most any child can memorize those words. But it is profound. Because if we can live with that kind of trust in God, it will absolutely change our lives.

Notes

[1] R. Maurice Boyd, "Punctuate Your Life," *A Lover's Quarrel with the World*, Ian A. Hunter, Ed. (Philadelphia: Westminster Press, 1985), pp. 25-26.

Chapter Twelve
The Protest of Hope
Isaiah 35

Charles E. Poole
Pastor, First Baptist Church
Macon, Georgia

The mother of the bride stands in the crowd and waves goodbye to her daughter. The lines of white shoe polish shout "JUST MARRIED" from the back windshield. The parking lot is thick with rice. The crowd is laughing and cheering. She is smiling back her tears and waving goodbye to her baby. Deep down inside she's afraid it isn't right. She's never said it out loud, but she just knows it won't last. After they get home, the father of the bride fiddles with a stray birdseed that landed in his hair. He squeezes her hand and says "Everything will be all right." It is the protest of hope in the face of worry.

A man gazes out the plate glass window of a third story hospital room. Last night the surgeon said if all went well he'd call after about an hour. They took her out at 8:30 this morning. It is 10:15. Their daughter stares out the window and says "Everything will be all right." It is the protest of hope in the face of fear.

They park at the out-patient building and head up the sidewalk. She signs him in. He sits down to wait his turn. He's never had a biopsy before. When they call his name, she kisses him on the face and whispers with a quiver "Everything will be all right." It is the protest of hope in the face of anxiety.

They have three tiny children and one huge house payment. They told him today that business was just too slow, and, as much as they hated to lose someone of his ability, they would have to let him go. That night, over the phone, his dad said, "Son, you'll find something. Everything will be all right." It is the protest of hope in the face of despair.

"Everything will be all right." "Everything will be all right" is hope's protest in a world where, sometimes, everything seems all wrong. Is "everything will be all right" a naive sedative that belongs to a less than honest optimism? Is "everything will be all right" a mindless wishful splinter of escapism? Or is "everything will be all right" a real word for the real world? Is "everything will be all right" too good to be true? Or is "everything will be all right" too good not to be true in God's world?[1]

The Bible is sprinkled here and there with the most outrageous, elaborate, reckless announcements that "everything will be all right." Some corners of the Bible take that "everything will be all right" line and set it to music that beats all you've ever heard.

Why, take Isaiah. Isaiah takes "everything will be all right" to the most ridiculous extremes you've ever seen. When Isaiah lets loose with one of his "everything will be all right" announcements, it just beats all you've ever heard. I mean, think about it. Isaiah says that someday blind eyes will see colors, crippled legs will run races, mute tongues will sing solos, and deaf ears will hear them.

Wow! That Isaiah could say "everything will be all right" and make you taste it and smell it and feel it and hope it!

Isaiah would have us believe that some how, some where, some day, some way everything is going to be all right. He exhorts shaky, trembling, wobbly knees to be still. He invites anxious, dread-full, heavy hearts to take courage. "God is coming," says Isaiah, "and when God gets here, everything will be all right." Isaiah would have us believe that some where, some how, some day, some way blind eyes will see colors and crippled legs will run races and mute tongues will sing solos and deaf ears will hear them. Isaiah would have us believe that sorrow and sighing will flee away and joy and gladness will come to stay. Isaiah would have us believe that ultimately, finally, everything really will be all right.

Isaiah stares into the face of pain, fear, disappointment,

and disease and lodges his outlandish protest of hope against
the mounting evidence for despair. Isaiah stumbles across the
rugged terrain of the real world like one of those front and
back sandwich-sign men. He carries an outlandish billboard
around his neck. Look! He is coming toward us. Read the
front of his sign. It says "EVERYTHING WILL BE." When he
walks past we turn to see the punchline on the back. It says
"ALL RIGHT." EVERYTHING WILL BE ALL RIGHT. Imagine
that!

Isaiah is carrying a sign that says "EVERYTHING WILL
BE ALL RIGHT." Isaiah is lodging his protest of hope against
the mounting evidence for despair.

Isaiah would have us believe that, "despite all the evidence to the contrary," God is going to have the last word, and
everything is going to be all right.[2] Isaiah pickets in front of
the door of despair holding aloft the sign of hope.

You and I read his sign, and we want to believe. But the
evidence for despair is so great. Life, after all, has filled our
mouths with a litany of words that belong more to the vo-
cabulary of fear than to the language of hope. It can be a little
hard to spell hope from the same alphabet that makes words
like Ahlzheimers, biopsy, A.I.D.S., leukemia, lupus, divorce,
unemployed and war.

It can be mighty hard to hold Isaiah's sign very high when
you're walking from a square green tent to a long black car
cradling a three-cornered flag for a young life too soon gone.
Isaiah's protest can be a might hard to hear over the rhythmic
beeps and blinks of intensive care artillery. Isaiah's poster can
be hard to grip in hands pierced and taped for the third of
twelve chemotherapy drips. It can be a tight squeeze to fit
Isaiah's billboard through the door of a nursing home where
one woman prays to live long while her roommate begs to die
soon. Isaiah is stumbling across the rugged terrain of the real
world wearing a sign around his neck and holding a poster in
his hands and singing a story from his lips and bringing a
word from his God. The word is hope. "God is coming, and
everything will be all right." Isaiah really would have us
believe that, despite all the evidence to the contrary, God is
going to have the last word, and everything is going to be all

right. We read his sign. We see his poster. We hear his story. And we want, oh, how we want to believe!

There is a singularly wonderful definition of preaching in Joseph Sittler's book *Gravity and Grace*. That marvelous description of the purpose of a sermon goes like this: ..."that's what a sermon is for: to hang the holy possible in front of the mind of the listeners and lead them to that wonderful moment when they say, 'If it were true, it would do.'"[3]

Isaiah has done that for us. Isaiah has taken us up to that wonderful moment. He has taken the holy possible and hung it right out here in front of our minds: The lame will run, and the blind will watch them! The mute will recite, and the deaf will hear them! There will be a highway to travel where nobody will ever be lost, or lonely, or afraid, or embarrassed, or ashamed. Sorrow and sighing will leave and stay away. Joy and gladness will come and not go! God will have the last word! Everything will be all right!

Isaiah has taken the holy possible and hung it right out there where we can see it. And we are left to say "if that is true, it will do!" If that is true, it is enough! If it is true that God will have the last word and that somehow God will bring us into His unhindered, uninterrupted presence, then that is enough. If it is true that God is for us, not against us; with us, not away from us; receiving us, not abandoning us, helping us, not forsaking us; if all of that is true, then it is enough. If that is true it will do. If that is true, then my weak hands can be strengthened, my wobbly knees can be still, my anxious heart can take courage.

If what Isaiah has spelled on his sign and said with his lips and brought from his God is true, then, it will do. It is enough.

I am convinced that it is true. I am convinced that, despite all the evidence to the contrary, God will have the last word, and everything will, some how, some where, some way, some day, be all right. Even as those words leave my hand and find their way across the page, I hear the word of caution: "This is a dangerous sedative. 'Everything will be all right' is the first step towards a lethargic, apathetic, 'by and by' postponement of action, service and ministry." I would once have offered such caution myself. But no more. The caution is not needed. One of the greatest wonders of grace, indeed one of the greatest mysteries of conversion, is that when we are most filled with the hope of what is "not yet" we are most driven to give ourselves in sacrifice and service to what is "right now." The hope of the not-yet drives us with courage into the pain of the right-now. It is simply an inexplicable wonder of grace that the hope of God and the gospel is not the sedative which becomes our excuse from the world, but rather the hope of the gospel is the truth which becomes our strength in the world. Isaiah's protest of hope does not lull us to sleep, rather, it frees us to serve. Isaiah's protest of hope does not lure us into safe cloister, rather, it drives us with energy into the burdens, challenges and demands of real life with real words, real help, and real hope.

In the fourth summer of his life, our son Joshua encountered his first yellow jacket. That night, as we tucked him into bed, he was "itching" the remnants of the sting. As I turned to leave his room, he voiced a ponderous theological inquiry. "Daddy," he asked, "why did God make 'waspes'?" While I was stumbling around for some response about pollination, Joshua answered his own question: "I guess God just wanted us all to git stinged."

Joshua's conclusion can be pretty easy to reach. Given the presence of so much sickness, pain, crime, and chaos in this world, it's pretty easy to affirm his toddler's assessment that "God just wanted us all to git stinged." We will all git stinged... Not because God wants us to git stinged, but because we live in a world where there are germs and disease and problems and sin. We will git stinged, not because God wishes it for us or sends it upon us, but because we live in a world where bad things can, and do happen.

The hope of the gospel never once promises us that we will be given sufficient magic to live above the pain, live around the pain, or live without the pain. The hope of the gospel promises us that we will be given sufficient strength to live into the pain, live through the pain, and live beyond the pain. And beyond the pain, says Isaiah, God will have the last word. Beyond the pain, everything really will, finally, ultimately, completely, wonderfully, be all right.

This is God's world. The God who raised our Lord Jesus from the grave will do as well in the future as He has done in the past.[4] This is God's world. God will have the last word, and some how, some where, some way, some day, everything really will be all right.

"If that is true, it will do." Is it too good to be true? Not in God's world. In God's world, "everything will be all right" is too good not to be true.[5]

This is the hope of the gospel. And it is true.

Move over Isaiah. We're coming to help you carry that sign. Make room Isaiah, we're coming to help you hope.

Amen.

Notes

[1] For the phrase "too good not to be true" I am indebted to Frederick Buechner, *Telling The Truth* (San Francisco: Harper and Row, 1977), p. 98.

[2] See Frederick Buechner, *A Room Called Remember* (San Francisco: Harper and Row, 1984), p. 35.

[3] This quote is in Joseph Sittler, *Gravity and Grace* (Minneapolis: Augsburg, 1986), p. 63. I found it quoted in Walter Brueggemann, *Finally Comes The Poet* (Minneapolis: Fortress, 1989), p. 162.

[4] See John Claypool, *Tracks of a Fellow Struggler* (Waco: Word, 1974), p. 101.

[5] See Buechner, *Telling The Truth*, p. 98.

Chapter Thirteen
The Faithful Word and the Faltering Voice
Isaiah 40:1-11

by Paul D. Duke

Senior Pastor, Kirkwood Baptist Church,
Kirkwood, Missouri

Some passages of scripture have been set to music in such a definitive way that we can never read them without hearing in our minds the music someone gave them. Once a text has been made to sing for you, it doesn't want to speak again, it wants to sing. The opening verses of Isaiah 40 are such a text. Many of us cannot hear these words and not hear the music of Handel's *Messiah*, which has its beginning here.

Do you remember how Handel set these words? When the overture itself is finished, the strings begin playing a quiet, stately pulse. Then the orchestra suddenly stops—as a pure, clear tenor voice, high above, sings three notes, simple, descending like a hand on a shoulder: "Comfort ye." The pulse begins again and the voice rises higher and stronger: "Comfort ye my people." Then with a new strength of assurance: "Saith your God, *saith your God*. Speak ye comfortably to Jerusalem, and Cry unto her that her warfare, her warfare is accomplished, that her iniquity is pardoned."

The orchestra stops again and the singer breaks in, dramatic as a man running into the room with unexpected news: "The voice of him that crieth in the wilderness, 'Prepare ye the way of the Lord. Make straight in the desert a Highway for our God.'"

Now the music quickens with new excitement and certainty, and the tenor begins to sing this impossible, wonderful vision: "Every valley, every valley shall be exalted, every mountain and hill made low, the crooked straight and the rough places plain." And when he sings of the valleys, the music lifts the valleys up. When he sings of the mountains and hills the music brings them down. And when he sings of the crooked, the music is crooked but then straight and clear and plain.

Like many of you I have heard *Messiah* sung many, many times. The most unforgettable performance I attended was in a church of which I was a member. Two of the soloists for that evening were imported professional musicians. The other two, including the tenor, were talented non-professional members of our church. What made the hour so memorable was the illness of the tenor. We all knew he'd been sick that week, that his illness had affected his throat. We wondered if he'd be able to sing. But he was there in his place. And when the orchestra finished the overture and began that quiet, stately pulse, he stood and opened his mouth to sing Comfort—and what came out was not comfort at all. The voice was raspy and cracked and excruciating. We wondered if he'd stop and sit down. The conductor looked at him with raised eyebrows full of permission, but he kept singing, cracking, breaking all the notes like vases. We all developed a sudden interest in our shoes. Everyone blushed and squirmed as he kept on trying to sing those impossible notes. On and on he tried for six torturous minutes. He sang about valleys coming up but they stayed low, and the mountains wouldn't budge for him, and by the end, to our assaulted ears, all the rough places seemed rougher than they'd ever been before.

He was a good man. In his right voice he could sing the piece beautifully. But on this night before all these expectant faces, he couldn't get it right, and he just kept singing. I'm glad now that he did. His public agony with these words has become a sign for me.

The vision set before us is glorious. But for people like us to give expression to this vision is very, very hard. Advent itself, for your information, is the hardest season of the year to preach. The preacher must announce that God will soon do a new thing. But the preacher doesn't know exactly what new thing is coming or how it will come or when. And worse, it's far from certain that the people want it to come. The message of this text, the message of the season, is directed to people who know themselves to be exiles, people who are not at home in the systems they're living in, people who haven't bought into all this, but are longing for the new Day of God. Here's the news: The power of God will come to dissolve this culture and all its structures and systems. Our degree of attachment to these structures and systems determines whether the Promise is good news or disaster.

And suppose it *does* feel like good news, suppose your heart *is* homesick for God's future, are you inclined to believe that it really will come? Or aren't you discouraged enough yet to assume that the way things are is the way they'll always be? Does anyone here expect a Day when nation won't lift up sword against nation, when the strong won't victimize the weak, when people won't take all they can get while others go hungry? Do you expect this to come? Or are you hunkered down to scratch out the best you can in a world you expect to keep turning as it is till it kills us?

When the prophet to the exiles first heard the command, "Comfort my people, Cry to them," he was baffled. He said: What shall I cry? All the people are like grass. We're all like flowers down here, pretty for a day, then we die. Grass withers, flowers fade. God look at all this death! Look at all these ruined hopes. Comfort *these* people? Who's going to believe that God has the power to change everything and is moving now to do it? How do we find the hope to believe that, much less comfort anyone else with it?

Guess what our text says to such a question? It says, "You get up. Get up and proclaim this Word.[1] Get yourself up to a high mountain and sing out the news." Lord, we can't, our voices will crack. *"Lift up your voice."*

God our hope is weak. *"Lift it up with strength."* But we're afraid. *"Lift it up, be not afraid. Say to the people: Here is your God."*

You and I are reluctant to bear witness to the power of God because we feel so unprepared. We've got our own fears, we've got our guilt. There's so much we haven't worked out yet. Who are we to say the Word of God to anybody? We don't trust our voices very much. But as usual we've gotten it all backwards. You never get ready to lift up the Word to your world. You just do it. Sounds like a Nike commercial, doesn't it? It's the Gospel according to Nike—just do it! Find your way to share God's Word of hope. You never get ready to lift up the Word. You lift up the Word—the Word makes you ready as you need to be. The fact that we get it wrong, the fact that we're guilty or afraid, the fact that our voices tremble or crack with our weakness is not the point. The Word of God's faithfulness to do a new thing—*that's* the point. We're grass, and oh, how we wither. But the Word, it stands; *it will be fulfilled.* The world won't care about any temporary beauty or temporary flaws in the voice of your life. But the world is desperate for the Word of what God has done and what God will do. Ready or not, lift it up and let it work.

Alexander McClaren was a famous British preacher. One day he learned that a university lecturer in science, a professed agnostic, had begun attending services at his church. McClaren wanted to reach that man, so he began to preach a series of sermons dealing with intellectual difficulties to faith, science and faith, doubt and faith. After awhile the man came to say he was committing his life to Christ. Talking with him, McClaren mentioned the sermons and asked which one it was that broke through. And the man looked blank. "It wasn't a sermon," he said. "There's an old woman who comes to your church every Sunday. She's always here. The other Sunday when she was going out of church she stumbled on her way down the steps, and I was there and I caught her and helped her down. She turned to me and said, 'Thank you very much. Do you know the Lord Jesus? He means everything to me.'" And the man went home, where the little word she had spoken grew and grew till it became the very Word of God alive in him.[2]

The world isn't waiting for eloquence. The world isn't waiting for a professional. The world isn't waiting for all answers. The world waits for ordinary, faltering voices to say the word of hope that they have. From there the Word will do its work. Lift it up. Be not afraid.

Of course, personal conversation is not your only voice. Your life can be part of a community's voice. We have a calling together to make a voice in the world, a voice to be heard not just here, but far, far away. Our hope is huge, vaster than our culture, bigger than our people. We are Baptist people and our tradition has long been that in various seasons we renew our commitments to a global witness. We pray for far-flung missionary voices in other cultures. We take an extra offering to empower those missionary voices. This is as it ought to be. Every community of Christ is called to get themselves up as to a high mountain and to cry the Word that reverberates far and wide. Prayers and gifts for the global work of the gospel are part of the calling to cry out the hope.

There are other ways too. There are social and political ways to lift up a voice. The new world God is at work to bring is a world of justice and peace. Being faithful to the Word of hope means becoming more publicly and more personally the advocates of these. And there are personal lifestyle ways to proclaim the Word—living with simpler, less materialistic commitments, loosening our attachments and sharing God's bounty. And there are local church ways, giving ourselves heart and soul to a fellowship of witness, helping in its local work of love.

Every way I have named of proclaiming the word is imperfect. Every instrument we've got for bearing the message of hope is embarrassingly flawed, like the man who sang *Messiah* with a broken voice. It has always been so. It was so even of the strongest, most famous voice who ever took up this text. A man named John, who made these words his life, who *became* for his time this voice crying in the wilderness to prepare the way of the Lord. Wasn't his voice flawed and far from perfect? You could say his voice carried a certain raspiness of rage that the Word does not require. You could say that something in John's voice was too sharp, too dry, that he never managed to express his news with the splendor and grace that it wants. But he knew this. He knew that only the One to come would get it right. But he also knew what it's high time you and I knew: that the Word does not command the perfecting of the voice, only that the voice we've got be lifted.

Our God is surely on the way to do a new thing. The new thing has already begun in Christ. The journey is already launched, we've already come far. Stretched out ahead of us seem to be many obstacles, detours and delays. But the power of God will lift up the valleys and lower the mountains and straighten what is crooked on the way. Including and especially our voices. If only we'll offer them, crooked and rough as they are, the power of God will lift them and use them and make them straight enough to serve.

Notes

[1] For this turning of the text I am indebted to David G. Buttrick in *Homiletic: Moves and Structures* (Philadelphia: Fortress Press, 1987), pp. 345-396.

[2] From an upublished sermon by John Gladstone, "Giving a Good Account of Ourselves," preached September 23, 1990, Yorkminster Park Baptist Church, Toronto, Ontario.

Chapter Fourteen
Who Bears the Burdens?
Isaiah 46:1-4

by Roy L. Honeycutt
President
The Southern Baptist Theological Seminary
Louisville, Kentucky

How do you bear your burdens? Who helps you conquer your adversities? Where do you turn with your burdens when you discover there is no one else to whom you can turn? What do you do when your deities fall and religion is no longer dynamic? Isaiah of the Exile reminds us there are two kinds of religious experience but with equally diverse effects. There is a religion which individuals must sustain; there is a religion which sustains persons.

Religion As a Burden To Bear: Isaiah 46:1-2
What do you do, where do you turn, and to whom do you go when your gods fall and religion fails? The legitimacy of this question is so far removed from most of our spiritual lives that even to reflect on the possibility may be offensive. Yet, religion can become a burden to bear rather than an experience bearing the burdens of troubled people. How does Isaiah address this question: are there times when deities fall and religion fails?

The Fall of Ancient gods
Both the biblical revelation and human experience validate humanity's theological fall. Few persons question our

mortal fall. For evidences of such fallenness embarrass us with their frequency and intensity. Admitted our personal lives spiritually collapse in a fall as ancient as Adam. Yet, few of us conceive of gods who fall. Isaiah, however, described the fall of ancient deities.

On October 29, 539 B. C. Babylon, conqueror of the Near East and ruler of Israel, fell to a coalition of insurgent nations. Bel-Marduk and Nebo his son were chief deities of Babylon. As national deities they should have protected the kingdom rather than depending on their devotees to rescue them from national catastrophe. For in the ancient world religion primarily served to meet the needs of the gods. Sacrifices provided food for the gods. Priests and people dedicated themselves to elaborate rituals designed to appease the deities and to achieve divine favor. Subservience to the deities and the practice of structured rituals assured no disaster would defeat the nation.

Contrary to the promises of popular religion, however, Isaiah's caricature of the fall of the gods epitomizes the failure of spurious religious experience. His satire is laughable but accurate.

> The worshippers are obliged to save their gods, for the gods cannot save themselves. Instead of the gods bearing their people at the time when ruin threatens to engulf the latter, they themselves require to be borne, they become a burden.[1]

How ridiculous to load the idols, so uniquely identified with national deities, on the backs of donkeys and cattle to rescue them from the terror of national destruction. Yet, historical evidence confirms the practice of hiding idols during times of battle. Nabopolassar, first king of the Chaldean dynasty (626-605 B.C.) designated a special area in Babylon where cities could store their idols for protection in times of national crisis. Sketches of the period portray priests leading donkeys laden with idols as they fled for refuge from an invading army.

Is the picture clear? This is the inevitable portrait of spurious religion. Such religion inevitably fails persons at the moment when we most need the power of authentic religious experience.

The Failure of Modern Religious Symbols

The fall of modern gods and the implication for us in contemporary society is confirmed by an array of evidences. Few if any of us have an idol on a shelf or table, firmly nailed through its backside to prevent it from falling. Yet, while we may not have idols carved of brass, wood, or stone we have symbols for religious experience which we treasure as intensely as Babylonian priests protected the idols of Bel and Nebo.

Symbols of our personal religious experience are legion. For some they may include the church itself and symbolic experiences such as baptism and communion. Many discover in denominational structures through which we minister a way of symbolizing spiritual commitment. Our understanding of religious vocation or calling may become a symbol for the reality of God's authenticating presence. Even our personal devotional lives may become symbols which encompass the breadth of our growing experience with Christ. Each of these is a legitimate mark of our dynamic relationship with the Lord. Such symbols may be uniquely positive. Religious practices and institutions can be symbols of God's unique presence. The question is not the reality of symbols but their nature and function.

Today, our experience is much like that of the Babylonians of the Exile. Some of our religious symbols are also falling. Unquestionably, it is dramatic to speak of the falling of the gods. Yet, this emphasizes the crucial nature of the circumstances which we encounter. For we are witnessing in our generation the breaking of old shapes and symbols of treasured religious experiences and denominational ministry. These have so characterized our lives at congregational and denominational levels we barely conceive of dynamic religious life apart from their reality. Yet, despite their previous contributions many treasured symbols are now crumbling.

We have yet to witness the emergence of new forms to supplant traditional symbols; but that this must occur is obvious. We need to replace the brokenness of old symbols with new symbolic expressions of our relationship with Christ. This is possible because of the power of our Lord to create new things from old forms. He promises to mend our brokenness and empower us to discover new ways of symbolizing our relationship of wholeness with him and other believers.

Or, if we do not create new symbols and religious structures, circumstances will drive us to redefine the nature of old symbols which give tangible evidence of our faith. Without such concrete symbols we cannot experience the dynamism of worship, ministry, scripture, mission, denominational cooperation, or other facets of our religious life. Religious symbolism is an authentic reality which we cannot ignore without radical detriment to our spiritual benefit.

When Does Religion Fail?

Religion fails when we confuse symbols with the reality of God. Atheism has never been, nor is it today a legitimate difficulty for authentic faith. Martin Luther once raised the question, "What means it to have a god?" And then answered, "Whatsoever thy heart clings to and relies upon, that is properly thy God." As J. H. Oldham wrote,

> In every instance there is in the last resort something on which a [person] depends and to which [one] gives [his or her] final allegiance. When God has been slain [people] find themselves driven to put something in his place, some object in which they can place their final trust, some idol of their own making.[2]

If we would dare test our commitment, the absolute loyalty of our lives, then ask this question, "What are the real driving forces of my actions when I am free to act as I wish?" Our answer will identify with startling clarity the gods we really worship. As Paul wrote, "you are slaves of the one whom you obey" (Rom 6:16).

Unless we are discerning in our discipleship even our most treasured religious experiences may become idolatrous. We dare not confuse one or more manifestations of God with the essence of his reality. For we are guilty of modern idolatry when we substitute one aspect of God's revelation for God himself. In studying modern communications persons often emphasize that the medium is the message. In religious experience the medium is always less than the message; for the reality of God is both content and substance of revelation, whatever the means of his self disclosure.

Should we succumb to this temptation of confusing God with symbols of his reality we may become like ancient persons who saw God's creative wonder, but rather than worshiping God the creator they personified some force of nature which they worshiped. "They exchanged the truth about god for a lie and worshiped and served the creature rather than the Creator, who is blessed forever!"(Rom 1:25).

Often we substitute a witness to God for the essence of his being. The congregation is not God, however much it may bear witness to his grace. The Bible is not God, despite its authority as the written Word of God. Charismatic religious leaders are not God, whatever their places of respected leadership. Systems of denominational ministry and cooperation are not God, despite their constructive role in spreading the Gospel. _God always stands above and beyond church, Bible, minister, or religious structures._ Nothing we conceive or comprehend, venerate or revere supplants the essence of God. As Voltaire once said, "the most beautiful of all emblems is that of God, whom Timaeus of Locris describes under the image of a circle whose center is everywhere and circumference nowhere."

When we confuse religious symbols with the reality of God himself religion inevitably fails. Gods made with human hands disintegrate. Dead deities leave us clutching the dust of forgotten duties and unfulfilled aspirations.

Religion fails when it becomes a burden to bear. Religion also fails when it becomes a burden to bear rather than an energizing and sustaining spiritual reality. Not only do we value contemporary symbols of personal religious experiences which we may idolize; unless we are mature in our commitments we may devote ourselves to a form of religious life which becomes an oppressive and burdensome end in itself.

Religious experience can become a burden which we carry rather than a dynamic force to sustain and to support us in our crises. Though we love and support our church, it should never be a burden. We treasure the biblical revelation, but the Bible should never become a burden. Our commitment to a spiritual calling is a sustaining force but it should never become a burdensome symbol of God's effective calling. However demanding, personal devotional disciplines should never become burdens.

Religious experience transformed by the reality of Christ's exhilarating presence is no burden to carry. It is an immense source of support carrying us through our deepest trials. If you doubt the validity of this assumption, look to our Lord who again and again pointed his disciples beyond a religious system which had become more nearly a burden than a blessing. Hear his caution:

> The scribes and the Pharisees sit on Moses' seat; therefore, do whatever they teach you and follow it; but do not do as they do, for they do not practice what they teach. They tie up heavy burdens, hard to bear, and lay them on the shoulders of others, but they themselves are unwilling to lift a finger to move them (Matt 23:2-4).

> Woe to you, scribes and Pharisees, hypocrites! For you cross sea and land to make a single convert, and you make the new convert twice as much a child of hell as yourselves (Matt 23:15).

A Religion to Bear Human Burdens: Isaiah 46:3-4

In contrast to the burdensome nature of pharisaic religion with its imposed burdens, hear the promise of the prophet from Nazareth:

> Come to me, all you that are weary and are carrying heavy burdens, and I will give you rest. Take my yoke upon you, and learn from me; for I am gentle and humble in heart, and you will find rest for your souls. For my yoke is easy, and my burden is light (Matt 11:28-30).

Standing in marked contrast to a religion that is a burden which we must carry is Isaiah's description of a religious experience which carries covenant people. He turned his word images literally up side down. Few Old Testament passages use language of such marked contrast in so a brief passage. The prophet reversed precisely those words which describe the burdensome nature of a fallen religion (46:1-2) to characterize a sustaining, invigorating religious experience (46:3-4).

Vs. 1-2	Vs. 3-4
1. You carry (*nasa'*)	carried from womb (*nasa'*)
the burden (*nasa'*)	I will bear (*nasa'*)
2. Loaded as burdens (*'amas*)	have been borne (*'amas*)
3. Cannot save (*malat*)	will save (*malat*)

Isaiah used seven verbs to depict God's support of Israel. Two point to the past and five to the future. Such religious encounter as Isaiah described can carry us, never becoming a burden which we must bear.

Past Experiences with God

Two participles describe God's sustaining in our past. The passive voice underscores we are the recipients of God's beneficent actions: "you have been borne by me from your birth" (v.3). The Hebrew word translated "borne" is from a root verb (*'amas*) which means to load something or to carry a load. Here, it figuratively describes the Lord who carries his people. Elsewhere, the Psalmist used the same word to characterize the Lord's sustaining power: "Blessed be the Lord, who daily bears us up; God is our salvation" (Ps 68:19).

Isaiah's second verbal description of God's care is equally graphic: "... Carried from the womb" (vs. 3). He employed a commonly used verb (*nasa'*) describing a variety of actions. Old Testament writers used the verb 655 times meaning to lift, carry or take. One of the more graphic uses of that verb is to describe water lifting up a ship, bearing it away on its journey. So God lifts us up and carries us every day; just as the ocean bears a ship.

Pointing to our common heritage, Isaiah reminds us of God's faithfulness in our yesterdays. From our birth he has carried us, lifting us up in every circumstance. Will God continue to do this? I cannot prove he shall. But we can and do live with confidence that his past trustworthiness validates our confidence in his future reliability.

When the false idols we have created begin to crash and the old symbols which once were so dynamic for our religious life are collapsing, we believe the God and Father of our Lord

Jesus Christ who has watched over our lives, sustained us through difficulties, and brought us to this moment will continue to be faithful. He who has been steadfast to this point will surely walk with us the rest of the way.

Anticipations of God's Sustaining Grace in the Future

Turning from the past, Isaiah clearly identified five verbal actions which describe God's continuing sustenance. Not only does he use incomplete verbs to describe the continuing character of God's action, he also uses a verbal form to suggest completed action or the finality of his concern. Further, he inserts the personal pronoun in each instance as though to emphasize God's unique initiative.[3] One could translate the verbs literally with the subject repeated: I, I will . . . .

"I, I will carry you" (keep on carrying you *sabal*)

"I, I have made" (perhaps, "borne" (ʿ*asah* or *mʿs*)

"I, I will bear" (keep on lifting you up *nasaʾ*)

"I, I will carry" (keep on carrying *sabal*)

"I, I will save" (keep on delivering *malat*).[4]

The Bible offers us a unique quality of religious experience to sustain us in every circumstance. I cannot prove the reality of this experience, I honestly confess. Yet, from the deepest recess of my being I profess with glad affirmation the sustaining power of my experience with Christ. What the future holds I do not know. What the crashing of our religious and denominational symbols will create I cannot fully determine. Yet, in every ambiguous and uncertain circumstance I stake my life on two qualities of God's action.

Turning toward the past, I know God is trustworthy. Continuing to trust him, I do not anticipate he will change, however much circumstances may fluctuate and persons may vacillate.

Turning toward the future, I stake my life on the promises of God which bear the resounding authority of his historical acts recorded in Holy Scripture. The same God who has already borne me in his arms, carried me through decades of vacillating circumstances will continue to act consistently in the future. Because of who he is (I am he, ʾ*ani huʾ*), Israel has been "borne by me from your birth, carried from the womb; even to your old age I am he, even when you turn gray I will carry you. I have made, and I will bear; I will carry and will save" (Isa 46:3-4).

Such confidence in God's dependability undergirded our family when I was a small child. When we faced most difficult family circumstances during the Depression of the nineteen thirties I vividly remember a tattered poem placed on the mirror of my mother's dresser.

> I cannot always see the way that leads to heights above;
>   I sometimes quite forget he leads me on with hands of love;
> but yet I know the path must lead me to Immanuel's land,
>   and when I reach life's summit I shall know and understand.
> I cannot always trace the onward course my ship must take;
>   but, looking backward, I behold afar its shining wake,
> illumined by God's light of love; and so I onward go,
>   in perfect trust that he who holds the helm
> the course must know.[5]

I believe those words are as true today as they were during those difficulty days of my childhood. They will be true tomorrow and tomorrow and tomorrow. Why? Because Jesus Christ is the same yesterday, today, and for ever (Heb 13:8). Such words continue to sustain believers during their trials because "We know that all things work together for good for those who love God, who are called according to his purpose" (Rom 8:28). We trust the future to our God believing "I am confident of this, that the one who began a good work among you will bring it to completion by the day of Jesus Christ" (Phil 1:6).

The options today are ours, just as they always have been our choices. Century after century demonstrates this abiding truth. Religious experience may become a burden to be borne; or, it may be a life sustaining force which bears believers through deep valleys where dark shadows fall and fear abides. Let us claim the promise of God's Prophet, Isaiah of the Exile, and through the presence of God's Spirit make of our religious experience a continuing demonstration of God's sustaining power in an uncertain era.

Who bears the burden? Do we make religion a burden to

be borne? Or, do we allow the Lord to sustain us? For, "surely he has borne our infirmities and carried our sorrows" (Isa 53:4).

Notes

[1] Claus Westermann, *Isaiah 40-66*, Old Testament Library. Translated by David M. G. Stalker (Philadelphia: Westminster Press, 1969), p. 180.

[2] J. H. Oldham, *Life Is Commitment* (New York: Association Press, 1959), p. 57.

[3] Since the pronoun is part of the verbal form separate pronouns are unnecessary. When they appear it normally is the writer's way of emphasizing the individual.

[4] *malat* means to slip away, or escape; hence, to deliver or save.

[5] Gertrude Benedict Custis, "A Song of Trust," *Poems with Power*, edited by James Mudge (Nashville: Abingdon Press, 1935), p. 196.

Chapter Fifteen
Look to the Rock
Isaiah 51:1-6

by Stan Hastey
Executive Director
Southern Baptist Alliance
Washington, D.C.

Freedom, it can be argued, is the watchword of the whole of salvation history. The Bible, from beginning to end, is filled with the wondrous good news that in wisdom and love God creates every person free, just as God the Creator is free. In Old Testament and New, the Lord of Israel and of the Church is the strong, liberator God who sets people free. Prophets of ancient Israel and Jesus of Nazareth himself came proclaiming this freedom.

Nowhere is this better seen than in Jesus' inaugural address back in his hometown of Nazareth, where his faith had been formed and nourished in the womb of Judaism. Taking the scroll of the prophet Isaiah on that Sabbath in the synagogue, he opened the book to the place that reads:

> The Spirit of the Lord is upon me, because he has anointed me to bring good news to the poor. He has sent me to proclaim release to the captives and recovery of sight to the blind, to let the oppressed go free, to proclaim the year of the Lord's favor (Luke 4:18-19).

And then, in one of the most dramatic moments of his entire public ministry, Jesus addressed the congregation, saying, "Today this scripture has been fulfilled in your hearing." Freedom—that was Jesus' watchword as he began his ministry.

Freedom—it is as well the watchword of our Baptist movement down through the nearly four centuries of our history as a distinctive people within the family of God. For more than any other, that single word—freedom—represents the genius of Baptists. We Baptists always have championed it: freedom of the individual conscience in matters of faith, freedom of the congregation to determine its own ministry in the community and the world, freedom of religion in the social sphere.

Now this focus on freedom did not occur to our Baptist ancestors in a theological or historical vacuum. They focused on freedom out of the deep conviction, rooted in Holy Scripture, that every person is born free and created in the image of God, and that every person must repent for oneself, believe for oneself, follow Christ for oneself, interpret Scripture for oneself, and yes, think for oneself.

For freedom of conscience, what our noble forebear Roger Williams of Rhode Island called "soul liberty," is at the heart of the good news of God in Christ. We Baptists always have known that genuine faith is voluntary. We Baptists know that God recognizes and accepts no other kind. We know that faith, in order to be faith, always involves the willful turning from sin and self to God, so that any instance of a compelled faith is really an instance of no faith at all.

Our Baptist ancestors knew this and so do all true Baptists to this day. Abraham Lincoln, though hardly a Baptist, knew it as well. On the eve of the Civil War, he delivered an address in the village of Edwardsville, Illinois, in which he spoke of the dehumanization of slaves in our country and anticipated the bloody division between the states that was about to break out. In his remarks, Lincoln asked, "What constitutes the bulwark of our own liberty and independence?" He then proceeded to answer his own question thus:

> It is not our frowning battlements, our bristling sea coasts, our army and navy. These are not our reliance against tyranny. All of those may be turned against us without making us weaker for the struggle. Our reliance is in the love of liberty which God has planted in us. Our defence is in the spirit which prized liberty as the heritage of all (persons), in all lands everywhere. Destroy this spirit and you have planted the seeds of despotism at your own

doors. Familiarize yourselves with the chains of bondage and you
prepare your own limbs to wear them.[1]

Like Lincoln's message to the nation, Paul's letter to the
Galatians had to do with freedom. Paul, who had known the
bondage of his own day's version of rigid religious legalism,
wrote this magnificent treatise, this Magna Charta of Christian
freedom, as some commentators have called it, to remind the
Christians at Galatia that their freedom was precious and fragile.
Their liberation in Christ was too important, he was saying, to
be set aside in favor of slipping back into their former spiritual
bondage. That is what he meant when he exclaimed, "For
freedom Christ has set us free. Stand firm, therefore, and do
not submit again to a yoke of slavery" (Gal 5:1).

My friends, we too must stand fast in freedom, a freedom
that springs not from the powers of this world, not from any
human government ever devised, but from the Lord of heaven
and earth. This freedom was formulated, not in the minds of
mortal humans, but in the heart of the One who is Alpha and
Omega. It was forged, not in the crucible of a national con-
stitution, but on the cross of Christ. Yes, ours, like theirs, is a
freedom too precious and too fragile to be neglected or cast
aside.

Yet in our time some Baptists seem to have lost faith in the
supremely liberating power of the gospel alone to draw women
and men to God and have begun to advocate instead that our
free consciences ought to be formed instead by those who
claim to possess a higher and deeper knowledge of God than
do ordinary believers. Some of them even advocate that the
propagation of the gospel must have behind it the power of
government to ensure its success.

Isaiah reminded his generation of Hebrew exiles to "look
to the rock from which you were hewn, and to the quarry from
which you were dug" (Isa 51:1b). The great Baptist pastor of
the first half of this century, Dr. George W. Truett of Dallas,
once pointed to that text and declared:

It behooves us often to look backward as well as forward. We
should be stronger and braver if we thought oftener of the epic
days and deeds of our immortal dead. The occasional backward

look would give us poise and patience and courage and fearlessness
and faith. The ancient Hebrew teachers and leaders had a genius
for looking backward to the days and deeds of their mighty dead.
They never wearied of chanting the praises of Abraham and Isaac
and Jacob, of Moses and Joshua and Samuel; and thus did they
bring to bear upon the living the inspiring memories of the noble
actors and deeds of bygone days.[2]

Now I would not suggest for a moment that we bury
ourselves in the mausoleum of our past, nor was Dr. Truett so
suggesting on May 16, 1920, when he uttered those immortal
Baptist words. Yet what he said that day from the steps of the
United States Capitol in Washington are words we need to
hear in our time. They are words we need to heed again.

For he spoke extensively that day of the human tendency
to rely on others, and particularly on government officials
blessed by officially sanctioned churches, to become the authorities of our faith. So he issued this warning:

In behalf of our Baptist people I am compelled to say that
forgetfulness . . . explains many of the religious ills that now
afflict the world. All went well with the early churches in their
earlier days. They were incomparably triumphant days for the
Christian faith. Those early disciples of Jesus, without prestige
and worldly power, yet aflame with the love of God and the
passion of Christ, went out and shook the pagan Roman Empire
from center to circumference, even in one brief generation.[3]

And then he concluded with this timeless injunction:
"Christ's religion needs no prop of any kind from any worldly
source, and to the degree that it is thus supported is a millstone
hanged about its neck."[4]

How can it be, then, that so many of us present-day
Baptists have strayed so far from such convictions?

Forgetfulness, that is what plagues us Baptists today. We
have forgotten where we came from and what our first prin-
ciples have been. We have forgotten that our earliest denominational ancestors were a despised, persecuted minority
sect, yet a relentlessly dissenting band who stood up to the
authorities of their day and declared, "Enough!" Enough of
the coercion of the free conscience by self-appointed human

authorities! Enough of a state-sponsored religion that squeezes the lifeblood from true faith! Enough of the notion, disproven in every age of human history, that God needs Caesar to accomplish God's mission on earth!

Yes, we present-day Baptists need to be reminded that we are constantly to look to the rock from which we were hewn.

Where is that Baptist rock? Is it Plymouth Rock in Massachusetts, with its enforced religious conformity, its suppression of the free conscience to ecclesiastical and colonial authorities unequally yoked?

No, our Baptist rock is not Plymouth Rock. Our Baptist rock on the shores of the New World rather is in the smallest of the American colonies, in Rhode Island, where three and one-half centuries ago Roger Williams and John Clarke and their little bands of freedom-loving Baptists found their refuge. Our rock is not in mighty Massachusetts, but in tiny Rhode Island. For it was there that soul liberty was recognized and protected by law during the formative stages of our nation's history. It was there that all religious comers, including Jews, were welcomed. Even those of no religion at all were welcomed in Rhode Island.

We need to look to the rock. We need to be reminded that those hardy Puritans who first set foot on the shores of America, while seeking freedom of conscience for themselves, all too soon refused its exercise to all others. We must look to the rock because it is all too easy to forget the terrible truth that these same Puritans indeed came to tolerate less religious diversity in the New World than they themselves had known back in Old England. We must look to the rock because we are prone to forget that these so-called seekers of freedom hanged Quakers and burned witches and banished true seekers like Roger Williams and John Clarke and Anne Hutchinson to our Rhode Island rock.

Where is our rock? It is in other places as well, such as Virginia, where our Baptist forebears steadfastly refused to submit to another established church, this one requiring licenses to preach and extracting taxes for the support of what our ancestors called a "hireling" ministry. No self-appointed human authority, they declared, would dictate to their free consciences. So they invited and endured beatings and lashes and imprisonment to keep bright freedom's holy light.

We, their posterity, must not, we dare not, despise what they achieved at such great cost.

So how can it be that we have strayed so far? How is it that we so easily neglect, even despise our heritage of freedom? "Destroy this spirit," Lincoln warned, "and you have planted the seeds of despotism at your own doors. Familiarize yourselves with the chains of bondage and you prepare your own limbs to wear them."

My friends, let the word go forth that some Baptists will not wear the chains of bondage. Like many of you, I have learned that my own children will not wear them. They refuse to wear them. For they are children of freedom.

Nor must their parents be willing to wear them. That is precisely what more and more Baptists are determining today. We are determining that we will not be bound by authoritarian pronouncements or authoritarian presidents or authoritarian pastors. For we are a free people.

What we will do instead is to look to the rock from which we were hewn. We will not do this, however, merely out of some antiquarian interest. Rather, we will look to that rock in order to fortify ourselves for the journey ahead.

And let us make no mistake about that journey. Like our spiritual ancestors in ancient Israel and Rhode Island and elsewhere, we journey with no guarantee except for the lively hope that God goes with us. Like Roger Williams' flight from Massachusetts in the dead of a winter's night into an unknown place he called Providence, our journey likely will be perilous and lonely. But undertake it we must. For a free people can do nothing less.

Noting the lamentable tendency of free people to lose sight of the source of their freedom during his presidential address at the 1988 annual meeting of the Baptist State Convention of North Carolina, Leon Smith quoted from Carl Sandburg's poem, "Remembrance Rock":

For we know when a nation goes down and never comes back,
when society or civilization perishes,
one condition may always be found.
They forgot where they came from.
They lost sight of what brought them along.[5]

I have an idea Sandburg knew Isaiah. And so should we.
For what is true of nations is no less true of denominations.
Look to the rock. Look to the rock. Amen.

Notes

[1] Cited in John Bartlett, *Familiar Quotations* (Boston: Little Brown and Company, Thirteenth Edition, 1955), p. 538.

[2] George W. Truett, "Baptists and Religious Liberty" (Nashville: The Sunday School Board of the Southern Baptist Convention, 1955), p. 538.

[3] Ibid., p. 19.

[4] Ibid., pp. 19-20.

[5] Cited in *Biblical Recorder*, December 3, 1988, p. 8.

Chapter Sixteen
The Suffering Servant and the Broken Christ: Four Songs, One Story

by Alan Neely

Professor of Ecumenics and Mission

Princeton Theological Seminary

Sigmund Mowinckel in his monumental study of the messianic concept in the Old Testament and later Judaism, *He that Cometh*, says: "From the very beginning of the Christian era the prophecies in Deutero-Isaiah about the special servant of Yahweh (*ebed YHWH*) have been applied to Jesus Christ."[1] Eight times in the new Testament the writers quote directly from the servant songs (Matt 8:17; 12:18-21; Luke 22:37; John 12:38; Acts 8:32f.; 13:47; Rom 15:21; and 1 Pet 2:22), and with only two exceptions (Matt 12:18-21 from Isa 42:1-4 and Acts 13:47 from 42:6 and 49:6) all the direct quotations are from the Fourth Servant Song, that is from Isaiah 52:13-53:12.

Allusions to the songs appear at least another eighteen times in the New Testament (Matt 3:17; 17:5; 26:67; Mark 9:12; 1:11; 14:65; 15:28; Luke 2:32; 3:22; 9:35; Acts 17:24-25; 26:23; Rom 8:33-34; 10:16; 2 Cor 6:2; 1 Pet 2:24f.; Rev 1:16; 5:6). The reference from the first epistle of Peter is of particular importance: "He himself bore our sins in this body on the cross, so that, free from sins, we might live for righteousness; by his wounds you have been healed" (2:24-25).

For even though students of the Old Testament generally agree that these hymns likely were not originally intended as messianic prophecies, the life and death of Jesus infused them

131

with new meaning and significance. The parallels between the servant songs and the life of Jesus are as undeniable as they are impressive.

When George F. Handel solicited from his friend and librettist, Charles Jennens, the scripture texts for *Messiah*, Handel's greatest oratorio—some would say his only first-rate oratorial composition[2]—the Fourth Servant Song served as inspiration for fives pieces of his final composition, Nos. 23, Aria, "He Was Despised" (53:3); 24, Chorus, "Surely He Hath Borne Our Griefs" (53:4, 5); 25, Chorus, "And With His Stripes We Are Healed" (53:5); 26, Chorus, "All We Like Sheep Have Gone Astray" (53:6); and 31, Recitative, "He was Cut Off Out of the Land of the Living" (53:8).

The passages known as the Servant Songs are found in Isaiah 42:1-4; 49:1-6; 50:4-11; and 52:13-53:12. Because of their difference in tone and theology from the rest of Deutero-Isaiah, many scholars believe these four poems were not a part of the original text, but rather formed a separate collection that was later incorporated into the prophet's writings. Moreover, Old Testament scholars generally agree these four hymns "speak of a special Servant of Yahweh," an individual Servant who in several ways is distinct from the concept of the nation Israel as the servant in Deutero-Isaiah.[3]

The First Song (42:1-4): Yahweh Speaks

What is the message of this song? The Servant is commissioned by Yahweh, anointed by Yahweh's Spirit for a specific task or mission, namely, to bring *mishpat*—usually rendered "justice;" or as Mowinckel translates it, "right religion"—to the nations.

Now "justice" may sound too anemic, and "right religion" too imperious. But a study of prayers from ancient Egypt, Babylonia, and Greece, as Abraham J. Heschel has noted, reveals a wide-spread, fervent hope that God will somehow see to it that justice is administered to the poor. The fact that this was a prevailing concern in other religions as well as in that of Israel most likely indicates the poor infrequently received justice at the hands of the authorities.[4] If Mowinckel's translation is sound, then "right religion" will doubtless include justice for the poor and the powerless.

This first song is unquestionably a hymn of faith, a hymn of confidence. It is the language of triumph, even though the approach of the Servant is unostentatious, his method gentle and affirming. Absent is any suggestion the Servant will be arrogant or domineering. The mission, nevertheless, will not fail, nor will the Servant be diverted or discouraged. He will establish justice in the earth. And so effective is his effort that the distant coasts wait for his intervention.

The Second Song (49:1-6):
The Servant Speaks and Yahweh Responds

Here the Servant projects his message to the farthest islands and peoples. He announces he has been chosen even before his birth by Yahweh. His endowment or natural gifts as well as the preparation and protection afforded him by Yahweh are noted.

The Servant then describes his explicit calling, and how Yahweh has been his source of strength. His mission, however, has become more than the establishment of justice. Now it includes the restoration of Israel, a task in which the Servant has apparently exhausted himself in vain.

His fall-back position is, nonetheless, one of faith. And as if he is talking to himself, the Servant declares Yahweh will ultimately justify all his (the Servant's) efforts. His mission will not be for naught, but this self-assurance is lacking; it sounds almost hollow.

In the first song, success is certain. The Servant will not fail nor will he be diverted or discouraged. In this second hymn, however, things have not gone well, and the Servant is clearly near despair. It is then Yahweh who responds. Though the Servant's mission has apparently proved fruitless in that Israel has not returned, Yahweh will entrust him with an even greater task, for the mission of converting and bringing Israel back to Yahweh is said to be too limited: "I will give you as a light to the nations, that my salvation may reach to the ends of the earth" (49:6).

The paradox here is evident. All of us have know occasions when success has resulted in one's being given a greater responsibility. But here is a case where the apparent failure by the Servant has led to a much larger assignment. It should be noted that "nations" here is not a reference to political entities, that is, nation-states. It is a reference to all the peoples of the earth. The Servant's new mission has universal implications.

The Third Song (50:4-11): The Servant Speaks Again

It appears to me this hymn should be divided into two parts with four stanzas. The Servant reflects upon his mission, and then he addresses his hearers.

Part 1

Stanza 1. Yahweh has endowed the Servant with ears to listen and a tongue to speak to those who are weary and beaten down.

Stanza 2. The Servant in turn has been insulted and abused. He has been beaten, spat upon. Even the hairs of his beard have been plucked out. Yet he has endured all these afflictions silently.

Stanza 3. Yahweh will help the Servant. His resolve and courage, therefore, are unflagging: his vindication is at hand.

Who then would be so foolish as to bring charges against the Servant? Those who have dared to do so will be frustrated; they will disintegrate like a moth-eaten garment.

Part 2

Stanza 4. Those who still are afflicted and distressed are then "exhorted to take heart, to trust in Yahweh." And this reassurance is followed by a stern warning to the cruel oppressors. Destruction will surely be their end. God will see to it: "This is what you shall have from my hand: you shall lie down in torment" (50:11).

Despite the injustice and suffering, all hope is not gone. Yahweh will ultimately vindicate the Servant, Yahweh will punish the oppressors. Even so, is not this third song less confident? Vindication is said to be imminent, but the Servant has, nonetheless, suffered repeated indignities. There is hope and there is stiff resolve, but they are linked with a warning and an implied imprecation, which suggests to me that the future is uncertain. Restoration and retribution will be realized, but when?   The triumphant assurance of the first song is muffled if not altogether disappeared.

The Fourth Song (52:13-15, 53:12):
Yahweh Speaks and the Hearers Respond
The response of the hearers is very familiar:

> Surely he has borne our infirmities
>   and carried our diseases;
> yet we accounted him stricken,
>   struck down by God, and afflicted.
>
> But he was wounded for our transgressions,
>   crushed for our iniquities;
> upon him was the punishment that made us whole,
>   and by his bruises we are healed.
>
> All we like sheep have gone astray;
>   we have all turned to our own way,
> and the LORD has laid on him the iniquity of us all
> . . . .
>
> Yet it was the will of the LORD to crush him with pain
> (Isa 53:4-6, 10).

This fourth song begins with a declaration by Yahweh (52:13-15) that the Servant *will* succeed; the Servant *will* be exalted, and many will be astounded, so much so that nations will marvel. Kings will be awestruck because that which is unimaginable they will see, and that which is inexplicable they will comprehend.

Those who have been hearers now become speakers, a chorus, as it were. "Who would have believed it...who could have foreseen this as God's work? For he [the Servant] grew up as a sapling out of dry ground (i.e., grew up in the most unfavorable situation—and for this reason is "stunted and wretched in appearance").[5]

> He had no form or majesty that we should look at him,
> nothing in his appearance that we should desire him
> . . . .

> He was despised and rejected by others;
> a man of suffering and acquainted with infirmity;
> and as one from whom others hide their faces
> he was despised, and we held him of no account.
> Surely he has borne *our* infirmities
> and carried *our* diseases; yet we accounted him stricken, struck
> down by God and afflicted (53:2b-4, my italics).

The Servant who in the first song was to be a purveyor and guarantor of justice is now lamented as one who has endured the cruelest of injustices; he was despised, wretched, disfigured, suffering the pain and death that they, the listeners themselves, deserved.

What has happened is difficult to understand. The Servant was not a mighty cedar, but rather a stunted sapling. He was not a lion or an eagle (figures used to eulogize Saul and Jonathan), but rather a weak and defenseless lamb. He commanded no one's respect, he turned no heads. Moreover, he was stricken with a hideous disease—possibly the meaning of the word is leprosy (from the Hebrew *negaᶜ* or *nuggaᶜ* in v. 8), and his death was that of a sinner; he was buried with the common criminals.

All these indignities, however, he suffered without complaint. Unlike Job, the Servant accepted his anguish and fate without a murmur. He dies without protesting his innocence.

But here is the enigma: "Yet it was the will of the LORD to crush him with pain . . ." (53:10). Herein lies the mystery. Yahweh appears as one who not only acquiesces to the suffering and death of the Servant; Yahweh apparently purposes it. Was it not Yahweh who was touted as the great Vindicator in the third song? How then can we comprehend, much less explain this role of consenting to the humiliation and execution of the Servant?

We need not tarry debating the adequacy of this understanding by the prophet. This is the world-view of the Bible. If the Servant suffered pain, rejection, and death, it had to fall somehow within the scope of God's will. For nothing happened that was not ultimately attributable to God. Totally absent from the Bible is the neat, rational compartmentalization of God's will into intentional, circumstantial, and ultimate categories. Equally outside the scope of the biblical authors are the concepts of accident, purposeless fate, or randomness. "It was the will of the Lord to crush him with pain . . . ."

Why this was allowed or how it was efficacious is not explained. Theologians since the first century A.D. have analyzed, debated, and systematized the biblical material and have spun out multiple theories of the atonement, such as the ransom thesis of the Anti-Nicene fathers, the satisfaction theory of Anselm's *Cur Deus Homo*, the penal substitutionary view of the Reformers, and the contemporary *Christus Victor* theory of Gustav Aulen. But despite nearly two thousand years of theological reflection, the mystery remains.

What is remarkable to me in this passage is the insight, yea, the conviction that the Servant suffered not for his own sins, but for the sins of others. The rejection, the scorn, the sickness, and the pain which the people should have borne were borne by him (53:4, 8, 12). Here is the heart of this ancient hymn, the unfathomable depth of vicarious suffering—the suffering of the innocent as a guilt offering (*'asam*) for those who should suffer for their own wrongdoing. But not only is it vicarious suffering, it is redemptive suffering.

The injustice of the righteous suffering for the unrighteous, nonetheless, eludes rational explanation. Possibly it is because, as Heschel says in his discussion of *mishpat* and *tsedakah*, "righteousness goes beyond justice."

Yet, like Psalm 22 which begins with a wail or lament only to conclude with a mighty exclamation of faith, so concludes this Fourth Servant Song: "Out of his anguish he shall see light; he shall find satisfaction through his knowledge. The righteous one, my servant, shall make many righteous, and he shall bear their iniquities" (53:11).

The suffering of the Servant and his death will be vindicated in the ensuing *righteousness* of his offspring. And it is this Old Testament concept of "righteousness," *tsedakah*, that forms the etymological and theological bridge to the New Testament understanding of the broken Christ.

Christ Made Sin for Us

In his second letter to the church in Corinth, the Apostle

Paul says of Jesus' death: "For our sake he made him to be sin who knew no sin, so that in him we might become the righteousness of God" (5:21). Do you understand this? Can you explain it? Though Jesus was himself free of sin, God put upon him our sin, that we might be transformed into the righteousness of God. Is this the act of a just God?

A Contemporary View of Fairness

Phyllis's remark to me was, I thought, half in jest, but we were talking by phone, and I could not be sure. What she said suggested the behavior of her sons was troubling to her, but even more troubling was what appeared to her to be the inequity of what was happening.

Let me say from the outset that Phyllis and her husband Ralph had been deeply involved in the church all their married lives. He had served in numerous positions in Baptist work in Virginia, and Phyllis was at the time the president of the local Baptist association and had served eight years as a trustee of the Baptist Foreign Mission Board in Richmond. You do not get any more involved than this, at least not in Baptist circles. Reflecting on their examples, the complete non-involvement of their sons was puzzling.

Her words to me that morning were, "God just isn't fair. God just isn't fair!"

"Why do you say God is not fair?" I asked.

"I know plenty of parents whose interest in the Church is at best half-hearted, and their children love the Church. Ralph and I, well..., we have devoted a good portion of our lives to Christian work, and now Jack and Phil will not 'darken the door' of the Church. I'm disgusted," she said, "and when I come back in my next incarnation, I am not going to be a Christian; I'm going to be a respectable atheist!"

The context of the discussion was, as you have probably already guessed, the unwillingness of their sons to "go to church." Though her latter remark about her next incarnation was obviously not serious, underlying her bewilderment was the feeling that God was not doing something that she, Phyllis, believed God ought to do.

Quid Pro Quo Theology

Have you ever had thoughts like this? Has a similar feeling or question ever bothered you? Is there a correlation between what we imagine we are doing for God, and what we can rightfully expect from God? Whether this question is psychologically consistent I am not prepared to say. But I do believe it is *economically* consistent, and a lot of contemporary theology is based on economic theory. We are culturally and theologically conditioned to think in terms of a *quid pro quo* relationship with God. This is one of the reasons at least that the idea from the fourth servant song is so troubling. "It pleased the Lord to crush him . . . ." The very thought that God was somehow gratified by Jesus' suffering is repugnant.

But *quid pro quo* or "tit for tat" theology has a very long history and respected place in Western religious thought. Is it not the basis for the theological system of merit? It appears to me that the idea that we can somehow earn and accumulate spiritual credit for the performance of noble and sacrificial acts is fundamentally an economic theory. Let me assure you, however, that despite the fact that Roman Catholics have systematized the idea of merit far more than Protestants, the doctrine of rewards and punishments, that one should and does receive from God what one deserves, oozes as well from every pore of *our* religious skin.

A Demerit System Revisited

Several years ago when our youngest child was in middle school, we were on furlough and living in Fairfax County, Virginia. Roger was doing his homework at the dining room table, and I was sitting just a few feet from him in the living room reading *The Washington Post*. He said to me, "Dad, what's a demerit?" I was not paying attention to his question.

"Uh, what was that?"

"What's a demerit?" he asked again. This time I heard him, and I can assure you from that moment Roger got my undivided attention. He got my attention not only because I was concerned that he had gotten into some kind of trouble at school, but more so because his question called up from my subconscious one of the most painful memories of my childhood, an experience I had not thought of in years. It was my memory of Rosemont Junior High School in Fort Worth, Texas.

I am not exaggerating when I say that the Rosemont Junior High School had a demerit system *par excellence*. Any violation of the rules, and there were innumerable rules, was punished by the arbitrary awarding of demerits. Every teacher carried in her or his purse or pocket a small pad of forms wherein the date, time, name of student, rule infraction, and the number of demerits assessed could be recorded. There was *no* merit system, only a demerit system, and the demerit system became my undoing.

Now the Rosemont school was a very elongated building with two floors, and from the second floor to the first there was a long, straight banister on the stairway. As you can imagine, it was absolutely prohibited to slide down that banister. Because it was prohibited, it was irrepressibly inviting, and one day when I thought all the teachers and other students were in their classrooms, I risked it. It was an exhilarating experience . . . until my feet hit the first floor and I turned around. For there was Ms. Lucille Burford, my general math teacher, not at all exhilarated. She was manifestly upset by my behavior. "Alan," she said, as she removed the record pad from her purse, "that will be four demerits."

Sometime later, Mr. Elmer West, my algebra teacher, caught me running in the hall. Running in the hall was also forbidden. "I'm giving you three demerits," Mr. West said in his most somber tone.

One day in early April several of us were coming out of the showers, and Eugene Stewart whom I had known since first grade was bending over, stark naked, to open his locker. The target presented by his posterior was irresistible. So I gave him a sharp pop with my towel. He "squealed like a stuck pig." Coach Herman Duncan had witnessed the whole incident and said that he was giving me ten demerits.

The following Monday, during the time the announcements were coming over the public address system from the main office, a secretary asked, "Is Alan Neely present this morning?"

Mrs. Smith, my homeroom teacher, responded, "Yes, he's here."

"Tell him to report immediately to Mr. Bateman's office."

Mr. Bateman was the principal. A clue to his demeanor can best be described by saying that Mr. Bateman never smiled. His reputation was: "Mr. Bateman tolerates no foolishness," and he could not have held more terror for me had he been the Spanish Inquisitor General Tomas de Torquemada with a black hood over his head.

I was ushered into Mr. Bateman's office. He remained behind his desk appearing stern and unyielding. Without looking up he growled, "Neely, do you know how many demerits are allowed before a student is expelled from this school?"

"No sir," I said.

"Fourteen," he replied. "Do you have any idea how many demerits you have?"

"No sir."

"Sixty-four," he snapped. "You are hereby expelled from Rosemont Junior High School. Clean out your locker and leave the premises immediately."

I walked home with the contents of my locker in a book bag, wondering all the way what I would say to my mother. Our family was poor, but we had recently acquired a telephone, and by the time I arrived, the school secretary had called and told my mother what had happened. I went in the front door. It must have been about 9:30 a.m. My mother was ironing in the kitchen and big tears were running down her cheeks. I know existentially about the demerit system.

God As a Celestial C.P.A.

Over the past several years I have become convinced that a *quid pro quo* theology is dished out in regular installments in many churches, so much so the average church attender probably conceptualizes God as an omniscient C.P.A. with a giant celestial computer. "I just earned 10 merits for going to worship." "That's nothing. I got twenty-five for working in the mission soup kitchen."

"Wow! Forty merits for attending the Holy Week ecumenical services."

"Oops. I just got 5 demerits for snoozing during the worship service, and I know Margaret got at least 20 demerits for getting so angry with her kids at the supermarket."

"I'm not telling anybody, but I probably got 75 demerits for lust when thumbing through the swimsuit edition at the barber shop!"

We are religiously and culturally conditioned to think in terms of "tit for tat." Capitalism has been with us for nearly four hundred years, and we instinctively think the accumulation of goods and wealth are necessarily, or should be, related to the production of those goods. One ought to receive what one earns, and one ought to earn what one receives. Charity and welfare are a disgrace. They stifle individual initiative and encourage deadbeats, spongers, and social parasites.

A *quid pro quo* theology also is evident in more than one theory of the atonement, but it is the fundamental underpinning of the idea of satisfaction. Why did Jesus suffer and die? Because of God's justice and righteousness. God could not be just and allow sin to go unpunished. Someone had to suffer, and that someone was Jesus. But what is suggested by the theory of satisfaction and what is thereby revealed in the cross is not God's inexhaustible love, but rather God's intractable, inexorable justice. The mercy of God is virtually obliterated by a demand for divine retribution.

The Biblical View of Fairness

"God just isn't fair!" Phyllis declared. In effect she was saying, "Years ago we established a relationship with God, and God has turned out to be an unprincipled welsher."

Most of us use these terms "fair," "just," and "righteous" in describing God, and our frame of reference is an economic context of capitalism and an established legal tradition of Anglo-Saxon common law. What we mean by the words, however, is something quite different from what the Bible means.

In ancient Hebrew *justice* and *righteousness* were associated not with the idea of treating everyone alike, that is, with being fair as we think of fairness, but rather with mercy, benevolence, beneficence, gentleness, forbearance, and compassion, especially toward the needy. One was righteous who eschewed avarice, bloodshed, violence, oppression, and tyranny.

Neither are righteousness and justice legal or forensic terms in the Old Testament. Rather they are concepts infused with personal meaning and implications for everyone who was a part of the covenant community. This is especially true in the prophets. Righteousness ensued not from conformity to an ethical or religious rule, but from a wholesome interpersonal relationship. One is also depicted as righteous who in a situation of estrangement moves into the breach and restores the alienated on to her or his rightful place within the community. Thus righteousness was evidenced in one's ability to redeem, reform, or rehabilitate another person.

In Deutero-Isaiah, Yahweh's righteousness is manifested not in the severe punishment of Israel, but in God's forgiveness and liberation of Israel (see 41:14-20; 43:3-7, 14-21, 25; 45:11-13; 47:4; etc.). Frequently "justice," "righteousness," and "mercy" appear in Isaiah, as in other of the prophets, in tandem.

In the New Testament, God's righteousness and justice are not revealed in God's ethical rigidity, but in rather in God's historical saving act in Jesus Christ in behalf of humankind wherein estranged and alienated sinners like you and me are brought into a covenant relationship. Our righteousness likewise ensues not from our conformity to an ethical norm, but rather from our trusting acceptance of God's salvific act in Jesus Christ. When we understand this, we are ready for the story that is frequently called "the parable of the laborers and the wages" (Matt 20:1-16), or as George Buttrick cleverly referred to it, "the parable of the eccentric vineyard owner."

Matthew 20:1-16: The Setting and Details are Strange

The story is about the harvesting of grapes, a task that cannot be delayed. It is about day-laborers who wait in the plaza to be hired, about the employed, the underemployed, and the unemployed.

During our last four years in Cali, Colombia, I never drove from the seminary to downtown that I did not pass a construction area where scores and sometimes more than a hundred men waited hour after hour hoping to get a job that would pay them a dollar or less a day. It was not unlike the setting Jesus describes.

The details of the story are no less disconcerting. The vineyard owner strikes us as a frenetic if not an impetuous man. He goes out and hires men at daybreak, then again at 9:00 o'clock, at noon, at three in the afternoon, and even at 5:00 o'clock, a mere hour before quitting time. Near sunset he says to his foreman, "Pay the workers their wages, but start with those who were hired last, and give everyone a full day's wage." It is as if he wanted to irritate those who had worked all day.

When the laborers who had begun at 6:00 a.m. and had worked twelve hours saw that those who had worked less were given a full day's wage, they naturally assumed that they would receive more. When they did not, they were rightly angry and began to complain bitterly. "This isn't fair! We worked all day, and you paid those who worked less, even those who worked only one hour, the same as you paid us!"

Jesus said, "The Kingdom of God is like this." Now, how does that grab you? "It isn't fair." No it is not fair if one imagines that the economy of God is one of *quid pro quo*.

"Do you mean you are going to receive tax collectors, known collaborators with the Romans . . . you are going to accept these whores, lepers, Samaritans, and common riff-raff as our equals?"

The vineyard owner's response: "Don't I have the right to do as I wish with my own money?" (20:15) is not an indication of divine capriciousness. It is, as one has said, an indication the economy of God is based on something far different from ours. Righteousness in God's economy is not manifested by economic or juridical fairness. It is revealed, in the words of an old Scottish theologian, in "the extravagant goodness of God." Neither is our salvation in God's kingdom the result of our performance. It is the result of God's unlimited grace. Who would have believed it?

One of the most provocative and most disturbing lines I have ever read is that spoken by Jean-Baptiste Clamence in Albert Camus' *The Fall*. The book is the painful, uninterrupted reminiscing by Jean who is haunted by his memory, a memory of a cold night when he was crossing over the River Seine. About midway across the bridge, he noticed a young woman standing seemingly staring into the dark water below. It was very late, and he wondered why she was there. Yet he said nothing.

As he reached the other side and continued on his way, he suddenly heard a muffled scream, then a splash. He knew immediately that the young woman had either fallen accidentally or intentionally into the river.

He had of course an initial impulse to return and try to save her, but he vacillated and then decided to go on his way saying, "Too late, too far." But he could not forget the experience; he never forgot it. Neither could he forgive himself, and the recurring memory of that moment of indifference finally drove him to the brink of suicide. Desperate for some relief, he contemplated going back to church. He had not been to church in years. But he would go and confess his terrible sin; he would do penance and somehow purge himself of his guilt. But just as quickly he discarded the idea saying, "No. No need to bother with that, for the Church believes solely in sin, never in grace." No point in seeking forgiveness, for the Church believes only in sin, not in grace.

When I read that line, I could not help but wonder if this were a commentary on my ministry, my Christian witness. If so, then I most of all stood in need of grace.

"It pleased the Lord to wound him," wrote the prophet. "He was made sin for us," declared St. Paul. But the broken Christ is not a symbol of penal justice. The broken Christ is a sign of divine grace.

"As far as the east is from the west, so far he removes our transgressions from us" (Ps 103:12).

This is not justice, it is grace.

"All we like sheep have gone astray, we have turned to our own way, and the LORD has laid on him the iniquity of us all" (Ps. 53:6).

This is not justice, it is grace.

"But God proves his love for us in that while we were sinners Christ died for us" (Rom 5:8).

This is not justice, it is grace.

"If we confess our sins, he who is faithful and just will forgive us our sins and cleanse us from all unrighteousness" (1 John 1:9).

This is not justice, it is grace.

Notes

[1] Sigmund Mowinckel, *He That Cometh*. Translated by G. W. Anderson, (New York: Abingdon Press, 1954), p. 187.

[2] Elwyn A. Weinandt says of Handel's works: "Many of the oratorio tests to which Handel wrote his music were second-rate in concept or execution, and sometimes in both. The poor quality of this vital ingredient weakened the pieces that resulted, and the problem of inferior texts continued to plague composers—especially in English—for several generations. [The] *Messiah* escapes this spate of mere words because its text is biblical, and its wide acceptance is, in great part, due to the strength and familiarity of the scriptural material. Without doubt, many others of his pieces would be competitors for its popularity if they were not saddled with what seems to us to be the inane libretti" (*Choral Music of the Church*, New York: Dacopo Press, 1980, p. 317).

[3] Mowinckel, p. 188.

[4] See Abraham J. Heschel, *The Prophets* (New York: Harper & Row, 1962), p. 200, n. 1.

[5] Mowinckel, p. 197, n. 1.

[6] "Justice," Heschel says, "is strict and exact, giving each person his due. Righteousness implies benevolence, kindness, generosity. Justice is firm, a state of equilibrium; righteousness has a substantive associated meaning. Justice may be legal; righteousness is associated with a burning compassion for the oppressed. When you extend a loan to a poor man, 'you shall not sleep on his pledge; when the sun goes down, you shall restore to him his pledge, that he may sleep in his cloak and bless you; and it shall be righteousness to you before the Lord your God' (Deut 24:10-13).

"It would be wrong to assume that there was a dichotomy of *mishpat* and kindness; or 'Justice was not equal justice but a bias in favor of the poor. Justice always leaned toward mercy for the widows and orphans'" (note 10 of Heschel, from R. Niebuhr, *Pious and Secular America*, NY, 1958, p. 92.) It is significant that particularly in later Hebrew the word *tsedkah* is linked with hesed, Jer 9:29; Ps 36:11; 40:11; 143:11f; see also Ps 85:11.) Divine justice involves His being merciful, compassionate (p. 201).

Chapter Seventeen
God's Power
Isaiah 52:13-53:12

by Thomas H. Graves
President, Baptist Theological Seminary
Richmond, Virginia

The issue of suffering and divine power has been a problem bedeviling humanity for ages. Job dealt with this question by refusing his friends' counsel that all the evil befalling him was punishment decreed by God. Paul struggled with the charge that he could not be God's true servant given the fact that he had suffered so in life. We remember the taunting of the crucified Jesus, "If you are the Son of God, come down from the cross" (Matt 27:40). To this very day there is spreading an Americanized gospel that proclaims health, wealth, and happiness to all of God's true servants, implying that those who suffer simply lack faith and therefore God's powerful protection. Elton Trueblood concludes that a great deal of religious difficulty "arises because of the fact that omnipotence is ascribed to God."[1]

The issue of divine power is one of the central questions of faith. Dostoevsky interprets the Gospel account of the temptations of Jesus as dealing with this crucial issue. In *The Brothers Karamazov*, the great Russian novelist retells the temptation scene in terms of three attempts on the part of Satan to have Jesus abuse his power. First, came the enticement to give people what they want by feeding them, then they will gladly follow you. Second, was the temptation to put on a show for the crowds by leaping from the top of the temple. If you dazzle the crowds with showmanship they will eagerly do what you ask. Third, was the boldest inducement of them all. Take up the sword of Caesar and force people by your own brute power into the kingdom of God. Jesus turns his back on such abuses of power. Dostoevsky, however, expands the story to describe a scene in which Jesus is confronted centuries later by the Grand Inquisitor, a representative of the established church. The Inquisitor, rebuking Christ for turning his back on Satanic uses of power, says, "We are not with you but with *him*: that is our secret. . . . we left you and went over to *him*."[2]

Is it true? Have we been on the wrong side for centuries? Has the fellowship of the faithful so misunderstood the use of power that we have acted as the agents of demonic forces? Is it true? Have we so perverted the use of our power that we have grown accustomed to the abuse of others and God's creation?

The topic of the use of Godly power warrants our careful examination. It has been asked from the time of Job and it was central to the ministry of Jesus. We are compelled to come to terms with how our faith tradition deals with divine power.

Nowhere else in scripture is the issue of God's use of power dealt with in such a beautiful and bold fashion as in Isaiah 52:13-53:12. This is surely the point of departure for any journey in search of guidance in dealing with the question of divine power.

Chapters 53-55 of Isaiah are the final chapters of a portion of scripture commonly referred to as Second Isaiah because they were written at a time and place far removed from other portions of this Old Testament book. These chapters date from the time of the Babylonian exile, a calamitous event which reduced the Hebrew community to political oblivion. The audience originally addressed by these words was in exile, in bondage, powerless, and captive. They had become pawns in the power struggles of nations. Throughout the works of Second Isaiah, one constantly encounters a mood of helplessness. Jerusalem lies in ruins and the very fabric of the people is torn asunder.

In such a desperate situation the natural cry from people is obviously for salvation from oppression and release from captivity. The popular vision of such salvation is often seen in terms of might and regal glory. A later generation of oppressed Israelites wrote of their hopes for release from Roman rule in the Psalms of Solomon. The words of that poetry express the common human desire for vengeance and force:

> Behold, O Lord, and raise up unto them their king, the
>   Son of David, . . .
> And gird him with strength that he may shatter
>   unrighteous rulers, . . .
> With a rod of iron he shall break in pieces all their
>   substance. . . .
> All nations shall be in fear before him (17:21-25, 39).

That is our common hope, that is our natural human desire. We feel persons who possess power should wield that power for their own protection and advancement. The Israelites under Roman rule or in Babylonian exile were no different. It is in this context of exile and anger that the words of Isaiah 52:13-53:12 were written.

The message of these verses is astounding. What we expect to hear and what we want to hear is that God's might and power will be revealed in the defeat of the forces of evil and the glorification of the righteous. However, Isaiah's description of divine glory and power is so unexpected that the author describes kings as falling silent upon hearing the news (52:15). Exactly what would it take to quiet all the politicians? Just this: a depiction of glory as identification with suffering and sorrow. Glory is described as weakness, vulnerability, and shame. The prophet himself asks, "Who has believed what we have heard?" (53:1). God's deliverance comes by way of one who is despised, rejected, ugly, diseased, and wounded. Isaiah describes divine glory, not in terms of regal and militaristic images, but with images of suffering; not in terms of angelic choirs singing praises, but in terms of one who is isolated and shunned; not in the language of beauty and strength, but in words that speak of sickness and death. God's glory is seen in the description of one who comes to suffer with all humanity. Isaiah redefines divine glory in terms of humility.

In the same fashion as Isaiah dealt with images of God's glory, the Old Testament prophet provides an entirely different perspective on divine power. In contrast to our popular models of status, prestige, and victory, the divine use of power is described as the ability to alleviate the suffering of others. The Suffering Servant of God is described as one who has "borne our infirmities, carried our diseases," who "was wounded for our transgressions, crushed for our iniquities . . . and by his bruises we are healed" (53:4-5). In this light, the one with divine power is no longer seen as the one with the greatest strength; rather it is the one who displays the perfect use of power for the benefit of others.

Charles Hartshorne discards the popular definitions of divine omnipotence in which God is seen as the absolute controller of all events and the monopolizer of all power. Casting aside these mechanical models of God's power, Hartshorne comments, "God does not, then, 'make' the world as a carpenter makes a table, with the alleged difference that his material is 'nothing' rather than wood; he leads the world as a father leads his children."[3]

Outside of St. Paul's Cathedral in London is one of the most expressive pieces of sculpture I have ever seen. Emblazoned on the small pedestal are the words "Our Father." Then the statue itself depicts a simple peasant child walking along with the lambs. That is, I think, Isaiah's image of God's power, not mighty force, but loving care.

In these verses Isaiah has revolutionized our interpretation of God's glory and strength. Glory is seen as humility and power is viewed as suffering service.

There is great debate in scholarly circles (as well as in some circles that are not so scholarly) as to the identification of God's servant described in these verses. Some see Israel or a remnant of Israel as the clear point of reference. Others depict an actual historical figure of the time. Many take this as a messianic prophecy with no precise individual being identified. It has been popular within Christian circles simply to assume that Jesus is the one described.

Those debates will never end and I would suggest that they may, in fact, be beside the point. The issue here is not so much the identity of God's servant but the description of the one who serves God. The point is not that Isaiah had Jesus of

Nazareth in mind as he wrote this passage. I doubt that he did. The point is that this passage describes the type of ministry that is also exemplified in the ministry of Christ and should be the hallmark of all Godly service.

It does seem clear that Christ adopted the model of the suffering servant as the pattern for his own ministry, It is simply not possible to understand the words and actions of Christ during the week of his passion without reference to this passage. How else do we interpret the words spoken by Christ as he broke the bread, "This is my body that is for you"? (I Cor 11:24). In fact, the author of John's Gospel quotes from Isaiah 53:1 as a preface to the description of Jesus' celebration of the passover with his disciples, asking again, "who has believed our message?" (John 12:38). John recognizes Jesus' legitimate claim to divine power and glory when he writes, "the Father had given all things into his hands, and that he had come from God and was going to God" (John 13:3). Having made the stupendous announcement that all divine power was in the hands of Jesus, John then offers the details of the very next act of Jesus: he rose from the table, took a towel and a basin, and washed some stinking feet. That is God's glory and power: humble service for others.

Perhaps the more crucial point of a study of Isaiah's words is not simply to discuss Isaiah's understanding of divine power or to identify the model of ministry exemplified in the life of Jesus. Perhaps our greatest need is to deal with our own use of power and to illuminate our understanding of what it means for us to function as ministers in God's kingdom? We too are called to the tasks of suffering servanthood. That means our ministry is grounded in a sense of our own woundedness as well as our own willingness to promote healing. Oh God, have we become so accustomed to the pathways of abusive power and self-glorification that we fail to realize that "we left you and went over to *him*."? Let us hear again the words of Isaiah calling us to humble service.

Notes

[1] D. Elton Trueblood, *Philosophy of Religion* (Grand Rapids: Baker Book House, 1979), p. 245.

[2] Fyodor Dostoevsky, *The Brothers Karamazov*. Translated by David Magarshack (New York: Penguin Books, 1985), 302.

[3] Vergilius Ferm, ed. *Encyclopedia of Religion* (New York: Philosophical Library, 1945), s.v. "Omnipotence," by Charles Hartshorne.

Chapter Eighteen
The God Who Suffers
Isaiah 53

by Bill J. Leonard
William Walker Brooks Professor of
American Christianity
The Southern Baptist Theological Seminary
Louisville, Kentucky

See Him there—the suffering Lord, agonizing in the garden, scourged by the Roman lashes, thorns pressed upon his
head, bearing and breaking under the weight of his cross. His
hands feel the pain of nails; his side is opened with the thrust
of a spear. See him there, dying in his suffering.

And hear again the words of ridicule: "He saved others,
himself he cannot save." He lifted others from their suffering—he reached out to those in pain. He was God in the
flesh—but he could not escape the horror of human suffering
himself. And *that* is a problem. Because messiahs don't suffer,
they conquer. God doesn't really feel pain, he alleviates it.
God could never be so weak. He is all powerful; he is in
control of everything.

And yet, centuries before Calvary, the longing prophet
Second Isaiah warned us of the unbelievableness of God's
Suffering Servant: "Who would ever have believed that it could
happen?" he asked. And Carlyle Marney writes, "Who could
have believed and anticipated that God's own prospering Servant would have been so marred as to seem inhuman. That
God's chosen people should be battered beyond identification."[1]

The first century Jewish leaders who stood at the cross

could not really believe it. The Messiah suffering! NEVER! Our messiah will restore the glory of David. He will bring in the golden age of the kingdom, the power and the glory for Israel. Give us the new David, not a Nazarene blasphemer dying on a criminal's cross.

The disciples could not really believe it. They wanted a triumphant, transfigured Lord. One who might clothe the naked, feed the hungry, defend the poor but who would also overthrow mighty Rome, establishing the kingdom and saving the best seats for his closest associates.

We often do not believe it—that God suffers. We spiritualize it. He knew the resurrection was just around the corner; he didn't really mean that God had forsaken him. He didn't really cry out as one deserted and alone. Give us a risen, victorious Christ who provides answers to all our questions, comfort and respectability for our service. Conquering and victorious yes, but we must never forget that this Jesus we call Lord was smitten of God and afflicted.

And there it is again, what seems to be the foolishness, the humility, the scandal of the cross. The weakness of the God who suffers.

What can we say then? Say he knows. Jesus Christ knows what it is like to suffer, to feel pain, to be desolate, to cry out in agony, "My God, my God, Why hast you forsaken me?" Say he knows, "Nobody knows the trouble I've seen, nobody knows but Jesus."

But it isn't just that he knows what suffering is like, way back there somewhere in the past. It is that he suffers—he still suffers. How can we live with the memory of Auschwitz and Hiroshima, of crusades and famine, cancer and death and not believe that God still suffers, that our sufferings are his sufferings.

However the writer of Isaiah may have meant those words, the church has taken them very personally: "Surely he has borne our infirmities and carried our diseases" (53:4). Does his suffering mean then that our suffering is taken away? That we never suffer? No! A thousand times no! It means that we do not suffer alone, we are related to the God who suffered for us and who suffers with us. And this suffering confronts us all differently.

Sometimes we suffer because life is like that. Suffering is thrust upon us. In disease, death, hurt, betrayal, sin and selfishness, even in innocence, we cannot, any of us, escape suffering because life will bring it to all of us. And what will we do? There are times when we help others, when we bring healing and hope to suffering people but try as we might, we cannot stop suffering from encompassing ourselves. Life is like that, no one is immune.

So what are we to do? Are we to cry out against God, shaking our fists toward the heavens crying, "Unfair, betrayed, rejected, God has fooled us!" Are we to face suffering stoically as if all of life, even its evil, were God's will? Or will we plead for a miracle which delivers us. Well, we may attempt those and other responses but perhaps, like our Lord, we must confront suffering with the realization that we live by faith in the God who suffers with us. Faith isn't just believing that "something good is going to happen to you;" it is believing that God is present when nothing good is happening to you. Faith is not merely expecting a miracle, it is also believing when there are no miracles, when only suffering abounds. I used to think that it took great faith to believe in miracles, now I think it takes greater faith to believe when there are no miracles—to believe that God is present when there is only pain and sorrow.

The Psalmist confessed: "Even though I walk through the darkest valley, I fear no evil, for you are with me" (Ps 23:4). So we confront the sufferings life brings to us—sometimes weeping, sometimes crying out in pain, sometimes with a sense of deep despondence, but always holding on in faith to the reality of God's suffering presence.

Thus at once we know both pain and hope. Martin Luther knew this paradox as he stood at the grave of his 14 year old daughter and acknowledged: "Magdalenchen, you will rise and shine like the stars and the sun, how strange it is to know that she is at peace and all is well and yet to be so sorrowful."[2] We weep, we cry out in our suffering, yet we confess that God is present with us. Truly he has borne *our* griefs and carried *our* sorrows.

Sometimes our sufferings are self-inflicted. We sin and bring pain to ourselves, our family, and our friends. And not one of us is immune from this experience of suffering. We are like sheep, we have all wandered, all gone astray, all followed our own instincts. In our common cruelty, in our subtle callousness, in our selfish desire to have things or succeed or gain power, we destroy others, we wreak havoc with goodness, we reject love, kindness and sacrifice. We want all of life, for ourselves, immediately. But often the visions of grandeur turn to nightmares, the power crumbles, the wealth is unfulfilling and the hollowness of our sin and the emptiness of our love descends upon us. Our selfishness brings only pain and suffering. What then? The word to us is that there is a way back from the self-inflicted suffering of our sin. Someone, some innocent one, some suffering servant has been wounded for our transgressions and bruised for our iniquities—there is a way back. The word from the cross is this: "Father, forgive them . . . ." In the midst of our sins and suffering there is forgiveness, wholeness and hope for restored relationships.

This suffering servant cries out at us that our sins are costly. This is serious business. Sin is not taken lightly; iniquity is not forgiven casually. It bruises and afflicts, it causes grief; it cuts us off from the land of the living. *And everyone knows the horror of our sins.*

But the suffering God does not merely condemn our sin and leave us to our indifference and self-pity. "He has been made sin for us," Paul says, "that we might become the righteousness of God" (2 Corin 5:21). "Upon him was the punishment that made us whole" (53:5). Let us reject forever the cheap grace of easy forgiveness and shallow reconciliation which denies the pain of sin and its consequences. But let us likewise reject the self-righteous cynicism which implies that none who *really* sin can ever come back. If there is no hope for the most blatant of sinners there is no hope for any of us.

The poison of our sins need not destroy us. God has suffered that we might experience the gift of reconciliation.

We can begin again. We really can. But suffering is not always thrust upon us by the cruelty of life; it is not always present because of our willfulness and sin. Sometimes, like Jesus of Nazareth before us, we must *choose* the way of suffering. Sometimes like Israel before us and like the Lord who has called us, suffering comes because of the way we have chosen, the way of the cross. When we identify ourselves with Jesus Christ, his sufferings and the sufferings of the world become ours. We become suffering servants. "Whoever would come after me, let him deny himself, take up his cross and follow me."

The cup of suffering which he drank, we must also drink. Thus we respond to issues, and events which may lead to suffering for us. Sometimes we must suffer innocently for truth as he did, not sinlessly, but innocently. We decide to offer ourselves for what is true, just and Christ-like and that may lead to suffering.

Jonathan Myrick Daniels was an Episcopal seminary student who, in 1965, went to Hayneville, Alabama, at the height of the civil rights upheavals in the South. On August 20, 1965, shortly after being released from jail where he was kept for his participation in a demonstration, Jonathan and some others had gone to a nearby store to purchase food. A white man with a gun appeared. Jonathan pushed aside a young negro woman with whom he walking and took the fire. He died immediately. The negro with him was told, "Nigger, you see what happened to him? You'd better get out of here now unless you want the same thing to happen to you." And when J. M. Daniels was buried some said, "How sad, how tragic. He should have stayed in seminary; he meddled where he should not and got killed for it. He was only a seminary student and he died before he ever got to be a minister." Others said, "Yes, it was tragic, but he was not waiting to become a minister—he died ministering to human suffering and oppression." Jonathan Daniels himself wrote: "Reality is kaleidoscopic in the black belt of the South. Now you see it, now you don't. The view is never the same . . . . Today the sun sears the earth and a man goes limp in its scorching. Tomorrow and yesterday sullen rains chill bones and flood unpaved streets. Fire and ice...the advantages of both may be obtained with ease in the black belt of the south. Light, dark, white, black: a way of life blurs, and the focus shifts. Black, white, black, a rhythm ripples in the sun, pounds in the steaming stinking shacks, dances in the blood. Reality is kaleidoscopic in the black belt. Sometimes one's vision changes with it. A crooked man climbed a crooked tree on a crooked hill. Somewhere, in the mists of the past, a tenor sang of valleys lifted up and hills made low. Death at the heart of life and life in the midst of death. The tree of life is indeed a cross."[3]

Sometimes we choose to suffer, to give ourselves in some way in response to the inhumanity and suffering of the world. And the sages are right: It is better to fail in a cause that will ultimately succeed, than to succeed in a cause that will ultimately fail. We may become the suffering servants one day and know the pain of misunderstanding and ridicule and derision. The cross belongs to all of us.

So the question comes: What sorrow and suffering do you carry today? Is there some hurt which life has uncontrollably thrust upon you or your family? Is there some pain which seems unbearable upon you or your children or others whom you love? Are you suffering for something in which you believe and for which you have been despised and rejected of men? Can there possibly be any meaning to all this pain? Perhaps. But it is not that suffering is good. It is that God, the god who suffered for us and with us, God is good. It is not that suffering has meaning, it is that love has meaning. And somewhere in the midst of even the most unbearable suffering there is God and there is love. Who would ever have believed it? That God suffers and loves us in our struggles and pain?

Perhaps that is what Second Isaiah the poet/prophet meant about Israel's servanthood and what the church believes about Jesus and his sacrifice. "By his bruises we are healed." Somehow, inexplicably, mysteriously in his sufferings, in his life, in his death, in his victory there is hope for all of us. Even if it is only the hope to hold on to faith in God when all else is falling apart.

Paul knew the presence of hope in suffering and wrote about it in II Corinthians:

> We are afflicted in every way, but not crushed; perplexed, but not driven to despair; persecuted, but not forsaken; struck down, but not destroyed; always carrying in the body the death of Jesus, so that the life of Jesus may also be made visible in our bodies. For while we live, we are always being given up to death for Jesus' sake, so that the life of Jesus may be made visible in our mortal flesh. So death is at work in us, but life in you (4:8-12).

The life of the living Christ is with us, even in the darkest places of our lives. So let us come once more to the cross and observe with trembling the suffering God—despised, rejected, wounded and bruised. And perhaps with him, in the midst of our own suffering, we shall be made whole. Who would ever have believed it? A suffering God! Hallelujah!

Notes

[1] Carlyle Marney, *The Suffering Servant*, 1965.

[2] Roland Bainton, *Here I Stand* (New York: Abingdon Press, 1950), p. 237.

[3] William J. Schneider, Ed., *The Jon Daniels Story* (New York: Seabury Press, 1967), p. 84.

Chapter Nineteen
A Hidden Mercy
Isaiah 54:1-8

by Scott Nash
Barney Averitt Chair of Christianity
and Chair, Division of Religious
and Philosophical Studies
Brewton-Parker College
Mount Vernon, Georgia

Chaim Potok's *The Chosen* tells of a young Hasidic Jew who is the heir apparent to his father, the Rebbe, or spiritual leader, of a group of Hasidic Jews who have immigrated to America and settled in Brooklyn. The young man is a genius, so intelligent that at an early age his father becomes frightened that his son's brilliance may lead him to be unsympathetic toward persons of lesser intellect. The father's solution is to subject his son to silence. Not complete silence. But almost total silence from the one whose companionship is most dear to the son, silence from the father, himself. Only when they engage in the Sabbath study of Torah will the father break the silence and converse with his son. Otherwise, theirs is a relationship without words, though each longs deeply for conversation with the other.

The silence eventually shapes the son's world, becoming at times so tangible he can almost feel its texture. The painful silence becomes his contact with the suffering of the world, sensitizing him to the hurting of others. He is drawn toward psychology as a vocation. He becomes a guide of the inner spirit, though not the kind he was "chosen" to be. The silence, in a sense, saves him, as his father hoped it would, and he comes to share his father's compassion as a tender of souls.

Isaiah's God tells a community of longsuffering Jews who are about to emerge from the long isolation of exile:

> For a brief moment I abandoned you,
> but with great compassion I will gather you.
> In overflowing wrath for a moment I hid my face from you,
> but with everlasting love I will have compassion on you"
> (54:7-8).

The sense of forsakenness experienced by these exiled Jews is not denied. The time of silence is acknowledged. The period of isolation is recognized as an act of abandonment and wrath on God's part. God confesses that for a while he has hidden himself from them. No explanation is given. Presumedly none is needed. The irrational causes of the experience and the rationalizations of why it occurred are already well-known to those who have endured. The moment's need is for insight as to how they should now respond.

The prophet's words are for those who have heard the sounds of silence and have walked hand in hand with loneliness. His words are for those whose eyes have watched the shadows suffocating the light of day, or whose hearts have felt the agony of loss, or whose dreams have all but died. They are words for our time: for the wife suddenly abandoned, the child bewildered by a parent's abuse, the browns and blacks denied society's benefits, the powerless among us and, sometimes, including us. They are words for those who know the experience of being exiles.

But the prophets words are also for those who do not know they are exiles. They are for those who abandon and abuse, those who have mistaken society's goods for ultimate good, those who are the power-stricken among us and, sometimes, including us. They are words for those who have accomodated themselves to a world estranged from God and have accepted the substitute powers as supreme. They are words that shock us into realizing that we are not at home.

The prophet's words acknowledge our estrangement from each other, ourselves, life, meaning, and God. They acknowledge for us what we often cannot acknowledge for ourselves. They describe life as it really is more often than we would like, more often that we dare admit. They admit for us that heaven is silent, shadows stretch across our days, emptiness fills our souls. They do not deny that beauty, justice, truth, and goodness are perverted, ignored, denied, and trampled. They confess that what we believe is contradicted by louder and stronger claims to veracity and value.

The prophet's words express what we reluctantly know and must confess to be true—that we are exiles, too. In countless and continuing ways as individuals, as nations, and as the human race we experience isolation and abandonment. We are hidden in a dark silence.

Isaiah's God admits that this is the condition of exiles. "I forsook you . . . . I hid my face from you." He is verifying a statement by J. Wallace Hamilton, a Presbyterian preacher of another generation: "Side by side with God's voice are God's great silences."[1] God's absence is a real part of our experience, so real that we are hard pressed to believe otherwise, so real that we desparately listen to those who speak on their own authority that it is not true, so real that we surrender ourselves to lesser gods. Exile is real for us, whether we can admit it or not. We have the prophet's word on it.

Yet, there is another word from the prophet. The dark silence of exile does not speak for all reality, only for the moment. The moment's experience is real, but it is not the only reality, nor the truest reality, even if it is the reality we experience most. Exile is real, but not eternal. Exile may even in a mysterious and ackward way enable us to experience that truer reality by sensitizing us to the everlasting compassion in the heart of God. Exile may, in a sense, save us.

What, then, must we do to be saved? The moment's need is for the insight to respond properly. The prophet has a word for this, too; in fact, he has three words, three commands.

The first command is, "Do not fear!" Why? "For you will not be ashamed ... for you will forget the shame of your youth" (54:4). Fear not because your faith is not in vain. Your God will not ultimately disappoint you. The God whose voice you have not heard in exile is the God who made you. The God whose presence you have longed for, whose touch you have almost forgotten, is the God who called you. This God is your Husband, your Redeemer, the Lord of Hosts, and the God of the whole earth (v. 5).

Isaiah's resume of titles recalled to those exiled Jews the God of their youth, the God of their past, the God of their mothers and fathers, the God of their songs and stories. The face of this God had become unfamiliar in exile. The gods of their Babylonian oppressors were far more familiar, far more tangible, far more real. The faces of these gods did not hide behind the silent darkness. They shone brightly and firmly from the gold-encrusted stone images in the pagan temples. Their omnipresent gaze peered from every structure and institution that shaped their lives: from the faces of their crown-headed rulers, from the shields of the soldiers, even from the coins in their purses. Political power, military might, economic infrastructure—they all confirmed the claims of other gods on their lives.

But Isaiah reminded them of another god, their God, the God known faintly in their faith. This God, hidden and silent in their exile, was present in their memory. They were being called back to their collective memories of this God to find assurance that they were not alone.

We are called back to this God, too. We are called to remember a cross on a hill surrounded by the silent darkness and the symbols of political, military, and economic power. In the memory of our faith there is an agonizing cry of abandonment in the face of a speechless heaven: "My God, my God, why have you forsaken me?" (Mark 15:34).

In the memory of our faith there is the assurance that this cry uttered in the silent darkness was not uttered in vain, that heaven did see and hear, that in that cry heaven was shining and speaking a word more powerful than the political, military, and economic idols which caused that death-cry. We are called to remember the face of the one who cried from the cross and to recognize him as the one who also cried from heaven, "Do not be afraid, I am the first and the last, and the living one; I was dead, and see, I am alive forever and ever, and I have the keys of Death and of Hades" (Rev 1:17-18). In this memory of the faith we are called to have faith, to fear not, to dare to believe that the dark silence speaks only for the moment and not for eternity.

Isaiah's second command is to "enlarge the site of your tent!" (54:2). Why? "For you will spread out to the right and to the left" (54:5). Isaiah's words here revive the memory of a time when the ancestors of those exiled Jews had experienced deliverance from another exile, the slavery of Egypt. He calls them back to the Exodus and the conquest of the promised land. He reminds them of the grand triumph of the past which constituted the beginning point of their life as a people.

But this memory is not recited as a wistful recollection of days gone by. It is proclaimed as a vision of days to come. The past functions here to provide a view of the future which transcends their present. They are being challenged to enlarge their vision, to see beyond those powers that shape their lives, to see "what is not yet but what will yet be" through the power of their God who creates and liberates.

The command is an invitation to redream what has always been an impossible dream. Frederick Buechner says, "It is madness to hope such a hope in our grim and sober times, madness to peer beyond the possibilities of history for the impossibilities of God."[2] He is right. It is madness. And, if we are not careful, this madness will get us into deeper trouble. If we let our hopes run wild and dare to believe that they are more than mere day dreams, we are setting ourselves up for great disappointment, great shame.

Still, we often run the risk of hopes run wild. We are prone to let our hopes run wild at the first sign that they may not be in vain. The demolition of the Berlin wall leads us to announce the end of the old cold war and the rise of a new world order. An apparent drop in drug use among American youths is seen as a victory of the war on drugs. The bombardment of Baghdad is heralded as the speedy resolution of the persistent Middle East problem. Our hopes do run wild, until we learn that such events only signal the onslaught of new, more difficult problems. Hidden hopes unleashed, then dashed by realism, lead to a doubting of the legitimacy of hoping itself. It is madness. Don Quixote should have been committed to the Old Folk's Home rather to have been allowed to run loose fighting windmills. Buechner is right. It is madness to dare to see the impossibilities of God in the possibilities defined by this world.

But Buechner is also right in wishing for more of this madness. Isaiah is right in calling for an enlargement of vision based upon the redreaming of ancient dreams, for these dreams are just as persistent as the realities which seem to render them impossible. The life of the community of faith hinges on daring to redream the ancient visions. As long as the community of faith permits the powers that be to shape its vision of what is possible, the power of faith itself shall be neutralized. The stone may as well remain across the door of the tomb. The exiles may as well make themselves at home in Babylon, as many Christians have done. We may as well grow accustomed to the silent darkness of exile, forgetting what faith might teach us in the depths of our exile experience. Isaiah's command is a dangerous one for it involves risk. But the risk must be taken if the reality of exile is ever to give way to that greater reality which has the power to transform us and take us home.

Isaiah's third command is actually the most extravagant of all. Perhaps, this is why he puts it first in his triad of commands for exiles. "Sing!" "Sing, O barren one, who did not bear; burst forth into song and shout, you who have not been in labor" (54:1a). Again, why? "For the children of the desolate woman will be more than the children of her that is married, says the LORD" (54:1b).

Without naming her, Isaiah takes the exiles back to Mother Sarah and her empty womb. Back beyond the Exile and the earlier Exodus, at the beginning of God's fulfillment of his promise to Abraham, the strangers of Babylon are led to rekindle the excitement that accompanied their miraculous birth as a people. "Laughter" was his name, that impossible child of two weary dreamers, Isaac, the child of promise. The aged pair had good reason to convulse with singing.

But, "How could we sing the LORD's songs in a foreign land?" (Ps 137:4). How, indeed, can exiles sing when heaven is silent and the world is dark? How can exiles sing when the dream is dead and hoping is hopeless? How can exiles sing when reality has removed the reasons, even the desire, for singing? Isaiah's first command is to sing. It is a brazen word, a presumptuous, cocky word. Walter Brueggemann has labelled this command to sing "a subversive act."[3] This act of celebrating an event which holds no practical promise of realization is a defiant challenge to the status quo. It is the final act of powerless people who refuse to accept the reality forced upon them by powers they cannot control. It is a proud act of stubborn rebellion. It is the supreme act of subversive faith.

This singing makes no sense, and yet we have heard the exiles sing: the song of slaves in the cotton fields, the poetry of Bunyan in prison, the prayers of Jews in concentration camps, the dancing of Palestinians in refugee camps, the marching of peacemakers in an American city. We have even heard the singing in some of our own songs, though not often enough.

In many ways, to sing of the end of barrenness when barrenness is all we have known is the ultimate act of faith. It is to trust a God we cannot see to do what cannot be done and to live as though this hidden God has already done the impossible. Buechner has described this act this way: "In a world with God, we come together in a church to celebrate, among other things, a mystery and to learn from, among other things, our ancient and discredited dreams."[4]

Isaiah's word here reminds us of Mother Sarah the barren one who had her hopes fulfilled. Isaiah does not name her, perhaps, because he is speaking to all the barren ones, all the ones who hope against the odds, against the possibilities of the present, against the silent darkness. He speaks to those who venture to believe, often only weakly, always foolishly, that the future is shaped by eternity.

In anticipation of an end to exile made possible by One who moves beyond the restrictions of reality, the faithful sing. They sing not because they have already experienced what they long for, nor because they are certain that they will, but because they are certain that the barrenness and the darkness and the silence are not the final words from God. They sing because they have learned that the silence was itself a cry of great compassion. They sing because in the emptiness of exile they have encountered a God who has himself experienced exile, a God who shares their pain of a silent heaven, a God who transforms the silence itself into song. They sing because in exile they, too, have been transformed. They sing because faith has taught them that the experience of exile was itself a hidden mercy.

Notes

[1] J. Wallace Hamilton, *Who Goes There?* (Westwood, N. J.: Fleming H. Revell Company, 1958), p. 107.

[2] Frederick Buechner, *The Hungering Dark* (New York: Seabury Press, 1969), p. 124.

[3] Walter Brueggemann, *Hopeful Imagination: Prophetic Voices in Exile* (Philadelphia: Fortress Press, 1986), p. 116.

[4] Buechner, p. 123.

Chapter Twenty
Non-Applied Religion
Isaiah 58:1-12

by Cecil P. Staton, Jr.
Assistant Professor of Christianity
Brewton-Parker College
Mount Vernon, Georgia

The alarm clock loudly signals the beginning of another Monday morning. John had thought about it a lot over the weekend. Now he kisses his wife and anxiously goes to his office at the brokerage firm. When he walks into his office he finds the unmarked envelope on his desk as promised. He opens it and discovers the expected information, insider information, illegal information. He has never done this before. He knows it is not right. And as he drinks his coffee the reverberating sound of the lesson learned as a child thunders through his head, "Thou shalt not steal!" He stares at the computer screen and knows that a few punches of the right keys will bring him more money in a few minutes than he could earn in months. Know one will ever know. His hands move towards the keyboard . . . .

It's Monday morning and Deborah backs out of the driveway and goes toward town. As she drives down the street she notices again the house with the wreath on the door announcing death. Her kids are screaming in the back seat. She is late for an appointment. She remembers this family was mentioned in her Sunday School class yesterday. "I don't have time to visit them," she tells herself. She knows they are new in town and wonders who has died. "Has any one stopped to comfort them? I wonder if they need anything? Someone else will surely see to it." She whispers a prayer as she drives on past their house . . . .

Stephen decides to begin his week by having lunch with his friend. No sooner do they walk out of their office than they encounter the same man they have seen before carrying a sign with the simple words, "I need a job. Unemployed for months. Children to feed." As they pass, his friend turns to the unshaven man in worn clothing, and with a loud laugh says, "That's right fellah. Why don't you go get a job!" As they continue walking Stephen remembers the sermon preached last Sunday about the hundreds of people who are unemployed and home-less in his city. He thinks of some work that could be done around his home. He would like to help. "It is, after all, the Christian thing to do," he muses to himself. But the voice of his friend still haunts him, "Get a job!" He dismisses the thought quickly as he continued down the street and enjoys lunch with his friend . . . .

"Non-applied religion." Is that how we would describe it? You know what I mean. We have all experienced this at one time or another. How are we to explain those moments when we do not do what we know our faith demands that we do, those times when we are confronted with human need and we fail to respond? For whatever reasons, our choosing not to act out our faith in a given situation occurs far more often in our lives than we would care to admit. As much as we hate to confess it, our belief, our faith, is at times no more and no better than non-applied religion, a religion sadly missing from our living. There on Sunday, but misplaced on Monday. We, too, are a people who "delight to draw near unto God," but a people who are too often unchanged by it. We are speaking of the strangest dilemma among the people of God, non-applied religion.

Non-applied religion is frightening. How often it is the subject of the scriptures. The prophets have a lot to say about it. Amos disturbed quite a few good religious folks when he told Israel that God said,

> I hate, I despise your feasts, and I take no delight in your solemn assemblies. Even though you offer me your offerings, I will not accept them, nor will I look upon them. Take away from me the noise of your songs; I will not listen to the melody of your instruments. But let justice roll down like waters, and righteousness like an ever-flowing stream (5:21-24).

Micah preached it in Judah when he dared to ask,

> What is it God really wants from us? Is it burnt offerings? What about young calves? Would the Lord be pleased with thousands of rams, with tens thousands of rivers of oil? Shall I give my firstborn for my transgression, the fruit of my body for the sin of my soul? He has shown you, O mortal human, what is good; and what does the Lord require of you but to be a justice doer, a kindness lover, and a humility walker with your God? (6:6-8, author's paraphrase).

Hosea sums it all up when he made it known that God's desire is for "steadfast love" and not merely the trappings of worship, "the knowledge of God rather than offerings" (6:6).

And here it is again in Isaiah 58. Maybe it could be ignored if there were not such urgency in the call of this prophet. "Shout out, do not hold back! Lift up your voice like a trumpet! Announce to my people their rebellion, to the house of Jacob their sins" (58:1). Look hard. You'll not find here a flimsy "I'll do it tomorrow," "maybe later," when I get around to it" indecisiveness in this message. The great prophet of the post-exilic age stands under the divine imperative to roar out to the people of God, "Your problem is a bad case of non-applied religion!"

Now lest we get the wrong idea, the expressions of belief criticized by the prophets were not wrong in and of themselves. The Old Testament prophets were not trying to do away with proper expressions of religious faith. Fasting, sacrifices, and religious assemblies were all perfectly legitimate ways of expressing one's faith in God in ancient Israel, just as legitimate as choir practice, Sunday School, and the morning worship service in any Baptist church.

Censured in Isaiah 58 is not fasting which the prophet implies, "can make your voice heard on high" (58:4). Their desire to draw near to God through fasting was a sincere and appropriate act of worship (Lev 16:29; Zech 8:18-19). The people addressed by our prophet were genuine in their desire to known God and his ways. They took pleasure in drawing near to God. They were puzzled when things did not go their way and even dared to ask, "Why do we fast, but you do not see? Why humble ourselves, but you do not notice?" (58:3).

Rather, the prophet criticizes God's people because their worship of God did not embrace the whole of their being. Fast days had become like any other day. Business went on as usual—quarreling and fighting. The bosses went to church while the workers remained in the field. And even when they did go to worship, they left unchanged by it. God's response was unequivocal: faith unlived is nothing more than non-applied religion. "Such fasting as you do today will not make your voice heard on high," the prophet declares. "Is such the fast that I choose . . . ? Will you call this a fast, a day acceptable to the Lord," God asks (58:4b-5)?

Non-applied religion rears its ugly head whenever our religion is only what we do on Sunday at church, whenever faith fails to become what we do at home, work, or school, with our spouses, children, families, among our friends, neighbors, and even strangers. The biblical witness is plain. Action directed toward God on Sunday must become action directed toward humanity on Monday, and every other day, or else all we have is a non-applied religion.

"What is the fast God chooses for us," the prophet asks? What outward expression of our faith in God is most appropriate for you and me? The only appropriate response to God's mercy and salvation is the fast of the whole being. Nothing less is called for than the sacrifice of the self which is dedicated to the purposes of God. Then and only then is the power of God unleashed whereby the people of God may become full participants in the divine activity which the prophet describes as loosening the bonds of injustice, freeing the oppressed, sharing bread with the hungry, bringing the homeless poor into shelter, and covering the naked (58:6-7).

Several hundred years after our prophets spoke their words, the prophet who had came to Jerusalem to die for the sins of the world would say to his small company of followers, "Just as you did it to one of these who are members of my family, you did it to me" (Matt 25:40). God's word through Amos, Hosea, Micah, and later Third Isaiah concerning non-applied religion now converges with the very challenge of the gospel of Christ: "We know love by this, that he laid down his life for us—and we ought to lay down our lives for one another . . . . Little children let us love not in word or speech, but in truth and action" (1 John 3:16, 18).

How significant this is for people of faith! The prophet tells his people that the results of a faith embraced through living are profound: "Then your light shall break forth like the dawn" (58:8). It is only when our worship of God takes hold of our lives that our light can penetrate the darkness of our world.

In Andrew Lloyd Weber's *Phantom of the Opera*, the Phantom allures Christine to embrace the darkness of his music and to love him in spite of his horrible face with the promise, "In the darkness it is easy to pretend that the truth is what it ought to be." We are a people of darkness. In the darkness of this world we find it easier to pretend that the truth of our existence is what it *ought* to be. It the darkness of drugs and chemical dependence, loneliness and broken relationships, pain and heartbreak, despair and death, war and conflict, the world pretends. How the darkness of our world needs Christians who embrace faith and apply it to daily living. Our prophet reminds us that a faith embraced will do for us and our world what non-applied religion can ever do. Then our light will burst through the darkness of this world, our healing shall quickly overcome us, and the very presence of our Lord himself will sustain us (58:8-9).

I tell you the darkness of this world will not be won to the light of Christ until what we say becomes what we do, until what we do in here in church becomes what we do out there in the world. Can we hear Christ's urgent call when he tells us, "You are the light of the world" (Matt 5:14)?

It is four o'clock and the bell announces the end of another trading Monday. The phone rings and on the other end a voice asks, "How much did you make us? I told you my information was reliable." John picks up the envelope from his desk and answers, "I'm sorry, but I just could not do it. I could not bring myself to do it." "Well I wondered if you would really do it. See if I give you any more information," comes the reply and the click. As John hangs up the phone he tears the envelope in two and drops it into the trash. Though the market is down and few trades have been made this Monday, John walks out of his office with the recognition of heart and mind and soul that his faith in Christ has taken another step forward.

The smell of freshly baked pound cake fills the air and is the first thing Deborah's husband notices when he comes in the door. "Would you mind if dinner is a few minutes late," she asks? "Not if it means I'll get some of that cake," he replies. "Sorry, I'm going to take this cake over to that new family down the street. I learned today that it was the elderly mother of the husband who died. I am going to see what needs to be done." Before her husband has a chance to say, "Of course," she is half-way out the door, feeling thankful for her family, her church, and her faith in the God of all comfort, realizing that her faith in Christ has taken another step forward.

Just as soon as Stephen returned to his office he went to the bulletin board. There it was. He thought he had remembered it. A replacement on the maintenance crew was needed. Now if only he could find the man with the sign. He walked up and down the streets near his building. Finally he saw him. "Hey, I think I've found a job for you. Would you consider working on the maintenance crew at my office." "Sure," the man replied. "I remember you. Thanks a lot." The forms were filled out. Stephen's recommendation was good enough for them. Was tomorrow too soon? "No problem!" Stephen took the man by the grocery store on the way to the small shelter where his family awaited his return. He couldn't help notice how the eyes of the unshaven man seem to come to life.

"Thank you," he said as he got out of the car with his bag of groceries. "I was beginning to think that no one cares any more. Thank you . . . ?" "Stephen," he said. "Just call me Stephen." As Stephen pulled away from the curb, he perceived something significant had occurred in his life that Monday. His faith in God had taken another step forward.

Boy, what a Monday! What will your tomorrow be like?

Chapter Twenty-One
Silence is not the Final Word
Isaiah 59:1-21

by Cecil P. Staton, Jr.
Assistant Professor of Christianity
Brewton-Parker College
Mount Vernon, Georgia

The silence of God—even the phrase sends shutters up and down our spines. It is a difficult subject for people of faith. Yet surely this is something life itself eventually will lead us to consider. We all endure this at one time or another. Yes, even people of faith sometimes find God strangely distant, silent, absent.

Life brings us times when, for whatever reason, God seems far way. Praise and worship come only with the greatest of difficulty, or not at all. Any prospect for joy evaporates. The light of life gives way to the shadows of numbness. Mysteriously death somehow reaches into the midst of life and threaten us. The long night of our winter of discontent does not give way to the much needed light of spring. We find that we are no longer capable of singing the song of life. Questions and doubt seem almost ready to overcome faith.

Though we know something is wrong, we find it difficult to explain. Though *we* may prefer *not* to articulate our feelings, fortunately the Bible has something to say about God's silence. For the Israelite theologians who give us the Old Testament there is nothing worse than the silence of God.[1] Yet at times they feel compelled to address this issue. Perhaps they are more honest than we are. Maybe they found some value in expressing their feelings forthrightly to God. Whatever the case, we are fortunate that the Old Testament preserves for us the personal testimony of some who have endured the silence.

Psalm 13, for example, reports the honest pleas of a soul in desperate trouble because God seems to have hidden himself. The pain of divine aloofness is brought before God through lament:

> How Long, O LORD? Will you forget me forever? How long will you hide your face from me? How long must I bear pain in my soul, and have sorrow in my heart all day long? . . . Consider and answer me, O LORD my God! Give light to my eyes, or I will sleep the sleep of death (Ps 13:1-3).[2]

The situation for the one who offers this prayer is critical. The hidden God must either come to the aid of the psalmist, or else the power of death will triumph over life.

At least a few contemporary persons of faith have also dared to address the silence of God as experienced in their lives. In a wonderful book called *A Grief Observed*, C. S. Lewis, the great Oxford scholar and tutor of a generation ago, candidly wrote of his feelings following his wife's death from cancer:

> Meanwhile, where is God? . . . Go to him when your need is desperate, when all other help is vain, and what do you find? A door slammed in your face, and a sound of bolting and double bolting on the inside.[3]

Most of us are probably uncomfortable with such honest reflection. But lest we take offense at these bold allegations against God, we must quickly remember that we are not listening to the ravings of the infidel and the blasphemer when we hear the words of the psalmist and Lewis. These are not the voices of faithless souls who in anger turn their rage toward God in a desperate attempt at retaliation. Rather these are the voices of people of faith, the reflections of honest faith seeking understanding.

The psalmist can lament the absence of God only because

God's presence has been genuinely experienced. God's silence is challenged because God has previously spoken. And anyone who has ever read Lewis knows of the great faith of this giant among twentieth century Christian writers. Yet a grieving Lewis is moved to ponder the provocative question, "Why is he so present a commander in our time of prosperity, and so very absent a help in time of trouble . . . ?"[4]

These are tough questions. But they are the questions of those who have known God's presence, questions of those who must now attempt to understand his absence. God's silence would not be at issue if God's voice had not thundered in the past. These are the prayers of people of faith—faith seeking understanding. C. S. Lewis' grief and the searching "How long?" of the psalmist reflect the common human experience of the silence of God.

Such a time also forms the background for the words of Isaiah 59. The post-exilic age was just such a time for those Jews who returned from exile in Babylon. They returned to Jerusalem on the wings of hope, a hope fueled by the promises of the exilic prophets. This hope is clearly seen in earlier chapters of Second Isaiah. Daringly the prophet declares:

> Do not remember the former things, or consider the things of old. I am about to do a new thing; now it springs forth, do you not perceive it? I will make a way in the wilderness and rivers in the desert (43:18-19).

> I will bring my deliverance swiftly, my salvation has gone out and my arms will rule the peoples; the coastlands wait for me and for my arm they hope (50:5).

> Enlarge the site of your tent, and let the curtains of your habitations be stretched out; do not hold back; lengthen your cords and strengthen your stakes. For you will spread out to the right and to the left, and your descendants will possess the nations and will settle the desolate towns . . . . For a brief moment I abandoned you, but with great compassion I will gather you (54:2-3, 7).

With such words to fuel their faith, the exiles of Israel made their way back to Jerusalem after the Edict of Cyrus in 538 B.C. No doubt they remembered the descriptions of

Jerusalem which their parents and grandparents had passed on to them (see Ps 137). The exiles were persuaded to trade their life in the comfort of the famous city of Babylon for the ruins of Jerusalem, still in destruction. What anticipation they must have had as they journeyed towards their ancestral homeland with the promising words of the prophets echoing in their ears.

Yet their hopes were dashed by the stark realism of that which awaited them upon their return: economic troubles (Neh 5:1f), famine and drought (Hag 1:10-11), enemy attack and opposition (Ezra 4:4; Neh 4:7f), discouragement, and apparently even the silence of God.

Where was God in all this mess? Had the Almighty abandoned those who made the long journey back to Jerusalem? Had God become deaf? Or was Yahweh the God of Israel now powerless?

To such a people and for such a time as this came a grace-filled word through God's messenger: "See, the LORD's hand is not too short to save, nor is his ear too dull to hear" (59:1). God's silence is not the final word!

From this point forward in Isaiah 59 we are treading on very dangerous ground. For Yahweh's prophet immediately turns to the explanation for God's silence: "Rather, your iniquities have been barriers between you and your God, and your sins have hidden his face from you so that he does not hear" (59:2). This raises a very perplexing problem. The difficulty here is that it would be unwise for *us* to conclude that in every circumstance the silence of God is due to human sin.

The Old Testament will never let us embrace this as a hard and fast rule. The story of Job rises up to crush our every attempt to equate God's silence with human sin. Oh that it were so simple! Job shouts out the objection for us all: "How many are my iniquities and my sins? Make known my transgression and my sin. Why do you hide your face, and count me as an enemy?" (Job 13:23-24). Life is not always so easy and *our* experiences will not always fit into the prophet's equation.

Nevertheless in this case the prophet is bold to declare God's explanation: "Because of their wicked covetousness I was angry; I struck them, I hid and was angry; but they kept turning back to their own ways" (57:17). In the specific case of post-exilic Jerusalem the prophet responds, "Need you ask? Your sins have hidden his face from you."

The sins of the post-exilic Jerusalem community were foreboding. The difficulties met upon their return apparently led them to embrace "their old ways," or presumably the very things which according to the prophets had led to the exile to begin with. Third Isaiah describes injustice, dishonesty, and violence. The whole community was contaminated by a pre-disposition to grope about in the darkness of social and spiritual depravity. Such was the community described by our prophet (59:3-8), who writes, "The LORD saw it, and it displeased him that there was no justice" (58:15b).

Moreover, all the while there was a wealth of institutional expressions of religion (Isa 58). Yet there was little in the way of what Yahweh really expected of his people. Their actions did not truly reveal a desire for relationship with God. God's presence was taken for granted when things went well. It was only missed when things got out of control. How could God speak at such a time as this? There was silence.

Be that as it may, the marvelous thing about this text is that the prophet's censure of his people's sin begins with a word of hope—a hopeful word for a people who have known the silence of God. Sin indeed builds barriers, divine-human barriers. Yet the good news must be heard even before the bad news is reported by this prophet of Yahweh. He begins with the grace-filled pronouncement that, "The LORD's hand is not too short to save, nor is his ear too dull to hear" (59:1). There is yet hope for sinners, even in the silence.

Having announced the grace of a God whose hand is not to short to save and whose hearing is yet unimpaired, the prophet reminds God's people of the seriousness of sin which always leads to broken relationship (59:3-8). Yet here we are also allowed to hear the people's confession of their sins. In this litany of worship sin is honestly confessed:

> For our transgressions before you are many, and our sins testify against us. Our transgressions indeed are with us, and we know our iniquities: transgressing, and denying the LORD, and turning away from following our God . . . (59:12-13).

The response to their confession is the prophet's renewal of the hope that judgment is but a prelude to a new act of divine grace. The announcement of pardon follows: "And he will come to Zion as Redeemer, to those in Jacob who turn from transgression, says the LORD" (59:20). God's silence is not the final word!

Biblical faith, real stout faith, honestly recognizes those difficult moments when the present God seems absent. Apparently questions about God's silence were honestly raised in ancient Israel and brought to God in prayer. Even in the midst of God's absence the people who had known God by experience clung to God in faith. The ancient Israelite prophet brings a hopeful word to the despondent citizens of post-exilic Jerusalem who recognize their sin and the barriers it creates: "The LORD's ear is not too short to save, nor is his ear too dull to hear." The prophet announces the good news (gospel) that God's silence is not the final word!

But there are also times when God's silence can not be traced to human sin, times when the silence goes unexplained. Psalm 13 makes no attempt to give a reason for this pray-er's plight. Yet the searching soul we hear in Psalm 13 concludes his complaint about God's absence with a declaration of faith in what will yet be, "But I trusted in your steadfast love; my heart shall rejoice in your salvation. I will sing to the LORD, because he has dealt bountifully with me" (Ps 13:6). In the midst of six brief verses this petitioner steps out of despair and into hope by faith. In this prayer of lament we overhear the prayer of a desperate soul who steps out of complaint and into the certainty that Yahweh will deliver. God's silence is not the final word!

Later in the same book C. S. Lewis would write,

> I have gradually been coming to feel that the door is no longer shut and bolted. Was it my own frantic need that slammed it in my face? The time when there is nothing at all in your soul except a cry for help may be just the time when God can't give it: you are like the drowning man who can't be helped because he clutches and grabs. Perhaps your own cries deafen you to the voice you hoped to hear . . . Turned to God, my mind no longer meets that locked door.[4]

God's silence is not the final word!

The silence of God—a frightening thought. Sin, grief, loneliness, despair—whatever our situation or whatever the cause even if it can be determined, these must give way to Isaiah's confession of faith in God's consummate word, and that word is grace. The final word is *never* silence. Judgment is but a prelude to a new act of God's grace. "The LORD's hand is not too short to save, nor is his ear too dull to hear!" Beyond the silence swiftly comes the grace. Thanks be to God! God's silence is not the final word!

In Christ the long stretch of God's hand has reached all the way to where we are. So much so that Paul can say by faith, "Who will separate us from the love of Christ? Will hardship, or distress, or persecution, or famine, or nakedness, or peril, or sword? . . . . No, in all these things we are more than conquerors through him who loved us. For I am convinced that neither death, nor life, nor angels, nor things to come, nor powers, nor height, nor depth, nor anything else in all creation, will be able to separate us from the love of God in Christ Jesus our Lord" (Rom 8:35-39).

Into the silence of our lives comes the prophet's welcomed words of assurance, "The LORD's hand is not too short to save, nor is his ear too dull to hear!" God's silence is not the final word! Amen.

Notes

[1] See further, for example, Pss 6, 10, 22, 27, 35, 44, 90, 130, and *passim*.

[2] C. S. Lewis, *A Grief Observed* (San Francisco: Harper & Row, 1961), pp. 17-18.

[3] Ibid., pp.18-19.

[4] Ibid., pp. 58-59, 73.

Chapter Twenty-Two
From Frustration to Faith
Isaiah 63:15-64:12

by *Tere Tyner Canzoneri*
Pastoral Counselor
Atlanta, Georgia

This is a sermon about prayer. It is not about just any kind of prayer, but about the prayers of desperate people who have prayed and prayed until they no longer know how to pray. It is about the agony of those who do not see the kingdom of God coming into their lives, who do not feel the healing of God's presence, but who struggle nevertheless in faith to understand their lives and their relationship with God. It is a sermon that at one time or another each of us must live.

I know about living with this kind of struggle. I know it professionally. As a pastoral counselor I listen to people who are consumed with pain and with questions about where God is in the suffering of their lives. Some of these people want a quick fix to their spiritual as well as relational, vocational and other problems. When no quick answers are forthcoming, they leave therapy. Often they have viewed their own mother and/ or father as a rescuer and do not want to learn that God is another kind of parent. It is human to want God to take our problems away. But when it doesn't happen, it takes faith to live with life's ambiguities.

I also know about such struggles personally. In the course of preparing this sermon I suffered a loss that moved the issue from an abstract intellectual discussion into the realm of grief and heartache. If we are honest, at one time or another, each of us struggles with questions about how God is present and active in our lives.

This passage in Isaiah is about praying in the midst of such struggle. The material is elusive to us just as it was to the persons to whom it was originally addressed. How does one get hold of these questions? How does one manage the feelings that are behind them? There is movement in the passage through different stages of grief. The people to whom the passage is addressed move from expressing their frustration to living in faith with their questions. What was that process? This sermon will look at the different stages of grief and struggle that are in the passage. In some ways the sermon— like our lives—is unfinished and remains in process with the questions.

In this Isaiah passage, the prophet speaks on behalf of people who were also struggling with such questions. The passage is written from the point of view of those who had returned to Israel after the exile but before the rebuilding of the temple. The country was devastated beyond their imagination. No longer was it the land flowing with milk and honey that they had heard of all their lives. There they were in a strange place that was supposed to be home, and they were clinging to God's promises, trying to understand why things were not happening the way they had expected. These were the people who had done the right things, who had followed the prophet back to God's land. Their faith had been courageous, or at least adventurous. They had gone to church, said their prayers, paid their tithes and taken a public stand that involved personal sacrifice. But it hadn't been enough.

And so in this context this prayer begins. The petition found in our text follows an accounting of redemptive acts God had performed in the past. Why were these people reciting God's past deeds? One possibility is that they were trying to elicit a response from God. Perhaps they thought God needed a hint: "Here, God, are examples of things you've done in the past that we think would be appropriate in our situation." Maybe they were even challenging God: "It is said that in the past you did mighty acts. Prove it. Show us such power." But as we know from our own experience, hints and threats carry little weight with God.

Another possibility is that they were reciting the list to remember for themselves just what kind of God it was they were depending on. They wanted a miracle. Could they count on God to come through? By remembering God's acts of redemption in the past they reminded themselves that God did have the power to change their situation and at least on some occasions had used it.

This brings us to the verses in which the struggles and questions of these people are presented. It is very important that this struggle occurs in the context of prayer and their remembering who God is. The kind of questions being asked by these children of Israel will never be resolved by abstract intellectual pursuit, but only in relationship with God and within a community of faith. I may not experience God's power or presence in my life today, but I remember when I did experience God's power or presence in the past. And I claim as my own the memories passed on to me by others, my companions in the faith, both living and dead, who also have experienced God. No, it is no futile gesture to recite the history of God's acts. It is armed with such memory that I dare approach God with my present doubt. It is informed by such faith that I ask my own unanswerable questions, that I plead with God for intervention.

Our Isaiah passage begins with questions: "Where are you, God? Why aren't you acting? In our recounting of past deeds we noticed that when you claimed children as your own, you saved them from their distress. You are our parent, why haven't you saved us? Since our history tells us you can intervene, why aren't you intervening for us?" (author's paraphrase).

These are very difficult questions. Whenever you come upon them in your own life, beware. Any answers you arrive at will leave you with as many problems as they solve. For instance, if God can intervene in human history and does, why is there so much suffering? Specifically, why do I and the people I love suffer? Has God not noticed my dilemma? If not, why not? Doesn't God know everything? If so, then does

God want me to suffer? If yes, then what does that indicate about God? Is God arbitrary? If so, is God reliable? Would God ever wish the suffering of innocent children no matter what good comes of it? Is suffering a test? A punishment? Is God's intervention dependent on some attitude or behavior on my part? If so, isn't that based on works rather than faith? Or if based on faith, why aren't the most faith-filled we know spared? There is no intellectually satisfying path out of this dilemma. There is at least one theologian who will argue each of the above possibilities. Others solve the dilemma by saying God cannot or chooses not to intervene in specific human situations. But if that is the case, how are we to understand that? These were the questions the Israelites struggled to understand.

In spite of all their questioning, one thing was not called into question. That was their relationship with God. The Old Testament rarely refers to God directly as Father. This passage does so three times. Whatever the explanation, it was not that they lacked relationship with God. Even when they cried of their abandonment, they continued to reach toward God. Even if God were absent, God was still their parent. Claiming that relationship, they begged God to intervene for them.

The intervention they wanted was an act of God's mighty power that would frighten their enemies and make everyone afraid to hurt God's people. "Tear open the heavens and come down so that the mountains quake. Do things never before seen." The request had a certain logic. They had returned to Israel to reestablish God's kingdom. As they had journeyed there their minds must have been full of stories of how God had demolished the enemies of their ancestors who had also worked to establish or maintain the nation of Israel. The prophet had told them they were the remnant meant to do God's will in that day. A showing of God's power would surely restore the nation of Israel.

The expectation does not seem so unreasonable. But it was not meant to be. How were they to live with the disappointment? Letting go of expectations, particularly those backed with religious understanding, does not come easily. These people were like us; they looked for an explanation that would allow their expectations, their current understanding of God, to remain intact.

They were so set in their understanding that they assumed God felt the same way. They refer throughout the prayer to the desecration of the temple and the city. It was as if they were saying, "We are humiliated. Aren't you embarrassed? Everyone knows that we are your people, that this is your city. You may not care about our reputation, but don't you care about yours?"

It's a familiar sounding prayer. Our wars, our causes surely are the ones God should bless. We assume our enemies are God's enemies. This is not only true of national causes, but also religious factions. Don't we each believe that we have the truest understanding of God's will and purpose? This is not meant to imply that we should not act on the faith of our convictions. I am my own priest and can interpret God's word for myself. But I must avoid the pitfalls of the above prayer. I must not assume that God's interests are the same as mine. Even if indeed I understand God's will for me, this does not mean I understand God's complete will. God's will for others puts them on different paths than mine. We are not the same people; our journeys will reflect our differences. My talents God will use one way. And someone I may personally disagree with or even dislike will be used by God for great kingdom purposes. We may disagree and within our own lives each be right. This is especially a problem when our points of view are in conflict. What do I do when that person's mission desecrates my holy place? What do I do with my anger?

One of the things we do with people we consider our enemies is to confuse the behavior with the person. It's interesting that we don't do that about ourselves so much, but we certainly do it about others. When we have sinned we know that God is displeased, but like these Israelites we cling to the knowledge that we are not disowned. We will acknowledge and value that God was present and working in our lives even before we knew God. Of our enemies we are less charitable. Do we dare call anyone God created God's enemy? No matter what a person has done, is that person excluded from God's love? No matter how God is grieved by a person's actions, did

Christ not die for that person too?

Again we are tempted to the mistake of the Israelites. We think that our relationship with God is about special benefits rather than about service. The New Testament does not say God's people will be recognized by wealth or military victory or even the answers to questions. It says we will be known by our love.

This is not easy for us. We tend to want somebody to blame for our problems. Our suffering must be someone's fault. This passage struggles with this question in an interesting way. As the people tried to understand their situation, they go back and forth between blaming themselves and blaming God. Listen to what they say, "It's your fault, God. You made us stray from your ways. You hardened our heart so that we no longer fear you. We sinned because you were angry and hid yourself from us. You withdrew and delivered us into the hand of our iniquity."

At first hearing these accusations are startling. My attention was especially caught by verse 5, "you were angry, and we sinned." That seemed backwards to me. Some translations soften this to read more like "You were angry but we sinned anyway." But most commentaries I consulted leave it in the first form. What could be going on? What understanding would bring them to blame God for their sin?

Maybe they were just passing the buck. The precedent goes back to Adam, "The woman you gave me caused me to sin." Which interpreted means "It was really your fault, God." Whenever possible blame someone else. The best defense is a good offense. Whenever possible turn the tables on your accuser. You've heard such admonitions. Maybe these people just disliked the feeling of owning their guilt. That could explain the back and forth: they were getting used to the idea of being responsible.

But there's another reason such accusations might creep into a questioning prayer. This one is harder to resolve. If God is sovereign, if God at least allows if not decrees everything that happens, then isn't all that happens at least partly God's fault? It's back to the question of when, where, and why does God intervene. God stayed Balaam's hand; God blinded the apostle Paul. If God prevents some wrong-going, why not the rest? The answer is supposed to be human free will, but what about Balaam and Paul? Was their free will violated? Does God have the power to overrule sin? If God uses the sin for God's own purposes how does that effect God's responsibility? They were angry at God for not intervening. Did they project that anger onto God and assume God was angry with them? We know God can be justly angry at us. But if God could intervene and doesn't, are we justified at being angry at God?

And what of the efforts to blame themselves? I think it was confusion about this that created the misunderstanding about God's anger. How does one understand God's anger? Is it like human rage: vindictive, cruel, withdrawing of love? I do not think so. But when I sin, I become estranged from God. If I know my sin is displeasing to God, I may think it is God's displeasure rather than my sin that created the distance. This would be especially true for people who experienced their parents or other authority figures as punishing in that way. Maybe acknowledging that their behavior was something that would cause God anger was the beginning of owning their own responsibility for their problems.

What is it they know about themselves? They say, "We are no different from other people, we behave like people who have never known God. We are so unclean that even our good deeds are contaminated. We no longer even pretend to call on God for help or to live as God's people. Cut off from God we are like withered leaves caught up in the wind of our own iniquity."

What does this mean? Are these the same people who earlier demanded that God acknowledge them? Are these the folks who held onto and claimed their relationship with God in spite of the evidence that God had abandoned them? What does their confession mean?

It is possible that they were acknowledging for the first time specific behavior and wrong-doing that had kept them outside God's will. But given what has preceded the confessions this seems unlikely. What it reminds me of is a kind of child-like or magical thinking that I frequently encounter with people who dislike the circumstances of their lives. If I am to blame, then I can fix things. If I can quit doing whatever it is I'm doing wrong, then my circumstances will change. Such self-blame is an attempt to be in control. For instance, if I am a child who is being neglected by my mother, it is much better to believe that I am a bad child than that my mother either can't or won't take care of me. If it is my fault, then I can control the situation by changing myself. Then I will get what I need from my mother. People apply this same logic to God. Things aren't working out my way because I've been bad and God is punishing me or teaching me a lesson. If I repent, or learn whatever it is I need to know, things will change. God will fix it for me so that I no longer have to suffer.

This is a tricky issue, for surely each of us continues to have sin in our lives, and surely the day will never come when we have nothing else to learn. But is it right to say that God brought this situation because of my sin or unlearned lesson? God allows me the consequences of my own actions, but does God allow the suffering that comes through no action of my own? Yes, God is present in my suffering and is transforming me through it, but did God cause the suffering or to teach me some lesson allow it? If I never sinned and knew God perfectly would I be exempt from suffering? Was Jesus? I cannot control God or even my own life, no matter how I live or behave.

So the confession may have been an attempt to control circumstances or manipulate God. But there is another level of understanding of this kind of confession. These Israelites realized they were not that different from other people, in spite of having been chosen by God. The first interpretation points to their shared sinfulness as something to be overcome. But on another level perhaps they have a glimpse of the messianic kingdom where all are welcome, where their chosenness is not a measure of status but a call to service. If God in Christ took on human form, do we dare hold ourselves above others in the human community?

And what is it we share with the human community if not our brokenness? Let's look again at verses 6-8, this time as a description of that brokenness. "We have all become like one who is unclean." Once we begin a path that leads us away from God, we begin to forget who we are. The longer we wait to be reconciled to God, the harder it is to remember. "All our righteous deeds are like a filthy cloth." Once we are separated from God, nothing is satisfying. Perhaps our good deeds are done for selfish reasons. Maybe they are being done as an attempt to return to God. But that happens in the heart, not because of good works. "We all fade like a leaf, and our iniquities, like the wind, take us away." Isn't that exactly how it feels? Caught up in our sin, our true self, that person God created and redeemed us to be, becomes more and more lost. We feel less and less alive. Sin left unconfessed and unforgiven accumulates until it feels like a force of its own. Without help we become lost to it. "There is no one who calls on your name or attempts to take hold of you; for you have hidden your face from us and delivered us into the hand of our iniquity." Sin is separation from God. It is our sin that causes the separation; it is we who forget or refuse to call out to God. Perhaps we are ashamed; maybe we don't want to give up the behavior. Maybe we feel so bad about ourselves that we can't believe God would want to help us anymore. "Yet, O Lord, you are our Father; we are the clay, and you are our potter; we are all the work of your hand." But God does not abandon us. In spite of it all these people do remember. They have not yet understood what the problem is, but at this point there is a change in their attitude. What kept them from giving up before they got to this place? It would have been believable for them to have despaired totally. But they had known God in the past. They had the stories. In some ways this made the pain of God's absence worse for they knew what they were missing. But it gave them the insistence to persevere, to believe some path to reconciliation was possible.

From the change in the tone, it appears they remembered the best path; it sounds as if they turned to God in worship. "We do not understand," they said, "but what we do know is that you are God and we are your children, your creation. Help us." At this point they recognize that all their begging, bargaining, denial, anger, all their attempts to control are useless. If change comes, it will come because of God. And the change, when it occurs, will be in them. They confess their sin and their need for God. Then they do an interesting thing; they repeat their original concerns about the city and they ask again their questions. "Will you hold back? Will you stay silent? Will you continue to punish us?" That the petitions and questions are still there shows that the petitions and questions were not the problem. The problem had not been in their questions but in their attitude about the questions and about God in relation to the questions. Therefore the chapter ends appropriately with the people still asking questions.

But if we look ahead to chapter 65 we can see what kind of answer God does make to them. God said, "I was always with you, ready to be found, reaching out, saying, `Here I am; here I am.'" God was there all along, missing them, waiting for them, sending them reminders of God's presence.

Why didn't they find God sooner? I think it was partly because they were looking for big, extraordinary manifestations instead of the still, small voice nurturing and guiding them. If we don't worship regularly, if we neglect the study of God's word, it is easy to look for the wrong things and miss where God is and what God is doing. One of the reasons to remember all God's past deeds and revelations—not just the ones that are flashy or suit our own purposes—is so we may recognize more quickly where God is working and being manifest in the present. We must be careful that our afflictions, our hurt, our anger do not lead us away from worship but rather back to it.

This does not mean we should deny the pain, hurt, anger. These must be expressed. But there are healthy and unhealthy ways to do so. I think one reason the people had missed God earlier was that they were caught in their frustration. It had become a barrier between them and God. But once they expressed their frustration to God and got it out of the way, then they were able to hear God's response: "Here I am." The scripture says that God had been saying that all along. But it was only after they had expressed their feelings in prayer and brought them into perspective that they were able to hear God. Their questions did not go away. They did not get that kind of answer. But they were changed so that they had the ability to live in faith with the questions.

What is it we can ask of God? How do we plead with

God? We express to God everything that is in our hearts and minds. It is only when we find a way to stop blaming enemies, God or ourselves, that we can discover a way to live responsibly in peace with the questions. It is only when we can hope in God's love enough to demand an end to God's silence, remoteness and apparent indifference that we can discover that the silence, remoteness and indifference are in ourselves. Amen.

Chapter Twenty-Three
God, Like a Mother
Isaiah 66:13-14

by Ron Sisk
Pastor, Tiburon Baptist Church
Tiburon, California

Preaching about motherhood isn't as easy as you might think. First, of course, there's our normal cultural hoopla associated with the institution. Motherhood is on its pedestal up there with the flag and apple pie. By the way, have you called your Mom lately? If you haven't, shame on you. She's sitting there by the phone, in the dark, waiting. Some go further in praise of mothers than others do, of course. My friend Burt sent his wife a dozen roses for every day she was pregnant with their first child. Two hundred, seventy dozen! He had them delivered to her room at Columbia Presbyterian Medical Center in New York. Patsy almost killed him. The nurses almost did it for her.

When I think of motherhood I think first of my own mother, as you think first of yours. Then I remember my grandmothers, my wife Sheryl's mother—women who made motherhood their careers and left me with indelible images of strength and character and compassion. All that's made even more poignant as we see young women in our church entering into motherhood with joy and excitement.

And then I think about the others. The two Bay area mothers who have abandoned their newborns in the past few weeks, literally left them by the side of the road to live or die by the charity of strangers. I read the statistics this week telling of the direct correlation between crime by adolescents and their presence in abusive families. I think about exposes like *Mommy Dearest* and *My Mother/My Self* and I remember how many of you have told me from time to time of emotional scars your mothers have given you. Scars some of us will carry to our graves. Scars some of us to our horror find ourselves passing on to our own children in their turn.

It takes a lot more than having a child, you see, to make a person a mother. Some of the very best mothers are people who have never borne children at all. As the prophet Isaiah reminds us, motherhood, properly lived, is a reflection of the image of God. Most of us don't think about God in terms of Mother very often. The Bible is basically a patriarchal book. Genesis does say male and female are created in God's image. But the Jews were surrounded by pagan fertility cults with mother goddesses. Those goddesses were notoriously immoral, and the Hebrews wanted to be careful to distinguish their faith from pagan immorality, so we get all the way to Isaiah before any part of the God of Israel is ever described as feminine. The prophet breaks the gender barrier by saying you see what God will do for you and me when you see a mother at her best.

God, like a mother, comforts. If your mother's done her job well, there's a sense in which she's always emotional home for you. Not that you never break away. Every mother worth her salt wants her children to take wing. But that she's always there for you when you need to come home. Have you ever watched a toddler just after they've learned to walk and are beginning to explore? They laugh and take a few steps, then look back to be sure that mother is there. They go on farther and farther away, giddy with the power of $30.00 Reebok freedom, bubbling with the joy of independence, till suddenly they trip and skin something, or they frighten themselves with their own bravery. And they head back hollering for mother's comfort as fast as they can go. It's no accident that after Ramon Salcido's murderous rampage in Sonoma he set off for Mexico to see his parents. And it's no accident that when they interviewed his mother she said in effect, "I don't know whether he's done what they say or not. I just want to see my boy again." Mother love is like that.

That's why the prophet compares God to a mother in

Isaiah. Israel has been unfaithful. The nation has been driven into exile and suffered exactly the punishment it deserved. And like a mother can realize her child has been terribly, terribly wrong, and love that child anyway, God says to Israel "I will take you back again. I will give you what you cannot give yourself. I will comfort you." So God says to Israel. So God, like a mother, says to you and to me. No matter what you and I have done. No matter how far we have fallen, no matter what mess you may be in today, even if your own mother has long since given up on you, God, like a mother stands ready to comfort. And that hint of acknowledged motherliness makes us bold to look for other ways the scripture shows us God is like a mother. God, like a mother, comforts.

God, like a mother, helps us see. Teaching and discipline are the ways. "Train children in the right way," Proverbs 22:6 says, "and when old, they will not stray." I know you find this hard to believe, but every now and then I dribble food or fail to lean over my plate or pick up my dirty clothes. And when I do Sheryl always groans, "that makes me so mad at your mother!" Even these days with both parents working and fathers playing a more active role, we still have a cultural expectation that mothers will do much, maybe most of the teaching. The book that's been popular this recently is *All I Really Need to Know I Learned in Kindergarten*. Frankly I think most of the really important stuff came earlier than that. Say your prayers. Brush your teeth. Flush when you're finished. Say please and thank you. Don't play in the dirt in your Sunday clothes. And most of those things for most of us came from our mothers.

So God, like a mother, teaches. In one sense all of Christian faith, the Bible, the church, prayer, everything is nothing more than God trying to teach you and me the basics, the things we need to know to live. Maybe that's why they call it mother church. I decided to enter the ministry when I realized the most important task in human life is learning how to live well. That, after all, is exactly why God sent us Jesus—to teach us by his example. That's why God lives inside Christians through the Holy Spirit, to be our teacher moment by moment. And those of us who follow him find again and again the lessons he teaches are the simple ones: love God, love other people, do your best, never give up. How many times have you gone through a struggle like I have only to pull yourself up, slap your forehead and say, "Of course. God's taught me that before. How simple. and how silly of me to forget. I'll remember next time." And how often has God had to teach you or me that very same lesson once again? The thing is, God does. Proverbs says "she opens her mouth with wisdom and the teaching of kindness is on her tongue." God, like a mother, teaches.

God, like a mother, disciplines. Scripture says those whom God loves he also chastens. Family therapy literature these days is absolutely chuckfull of the assertion one of the things children need most in order to make a successful adjustment to life is consistent, fair, enforced and enforceable discipline. Very often the kids I feel sorriest for in our church are not the ones who have to toe the line. I feel sorriest for the ones who seem to have the most freedom, whose parents seem to pay the least attention to where they are and what they're doing. Or even worse, whose parents seem to have given up trying to make their standards stick. Some of our teenagers think they have it rough at home. That their parents are too strict. A good mother does give more and more freedom as you're able to handle it. But, you know, till I went away to college I never left the house without Mother saying, "Where are you going, Son? And when do you plan to be home?" And you know what else? That's one of my very best memories. That's one of the ways I knew that Mother cared.

God, like a mother, disciplines, my friends. God's set the standard for your life and mine. He's written the rules here in the book, plain for everybody to see. Made them flexible enough to be realistic and strict enough to be effective. Taught us how to walk. Told us how not to get our fingers burned. Let us know you can't play in the dirt without some of it rubbing off on you. Told us that he cares about us and that's the reason he's given us healthy boundaries. And sent us out to see how well you and I can do. Like a wise mother God sends us into life to let you and me experience the consequences of our own actions. Because some kids never learn to keep their hands out of the fire till you give them the chance to get burned. You may be in church today precisely because you got burned out there. And you're looking for a chance to start over. Well, hear the good news, my friend. Nobody's ever done anything bad enough God wouldn't give them a second chance. God, like a mother, disciplines.

God, like a mother, defends. "The hand of the Lord is with his servants, and his indignation is against his enemies." The picture ripped my heart out. It was in one of our denominational magazines not long ago. A Baptist mother in a Texas hospital with her hand on the brow of her son who was dying of AIDS. She had the kind of quiet dignity the best older women seem to show. Well-groomed, carefully dressed. No sign of overt emotion. But lines of pain in her face that shouted, "This is my son, and I can do nothing for him. This is my own and I would do anything, anything to save him from this end." In the face of an American mother watching by a hospital bed. In the posture of an Afghan refugee clinging to her child as she flees from the guns of Jalalabad. In the hopeless protest of New York City women, their sons accused of brutal rape and beating in Central Park, as they look at the news cameras in bewilderment and cry, "Oh, no, it can't be. Not my boy. He's a good boy, my boy. My son would never do such a thing." Translate it into any culture you like. Show the children as innocent victims of tragedy or willing participants in sin, but the mother's response is the same. A mother defends her children.

God, like a mother, defends. It's easy for most of us, I think to look at all this a little cynically. We've all known mothers who gave up on their children. We've all known children we thought deserved to be given up on. Still it's true. In the defense of her children, a mother does no more than reflect the image of God. God whom you and I, his children, have bitterly disappointed. God who from the vastness of eternity cast about the reaches of the universe for some way, any way at all, to defend you and me from ourselves. God who with all of a father's righteousness and all of a mother's fierce love could find no way to help his wayward children but to sacrifice the one who had never strayed. God who tore his own heart out sending Jesus to die for you and me, because God, like a mother, defends.

Some of us get mothering in the best possible way from the moment our first cry fills the air. Others of us spend all our lives hungering for a mother's embracing love. Most of us have mothers who do their best, helping us in some ways, hurting us in others. But the good news is the God you and I know most of the time as Father is bigger than human understanding. The good news is God who knows how to give us everything we need. Not just fathering the way fathering should be, but mothering the way mothering should be as well. Maybe even the very mothering you crave. "As one whom his mother comforts, so I will comfort you."